20/20

20/20

20 New Sounds of the 20th Century

William Duckworth

SCHIRMER

™

THOMSON LEARNING

Australia • Canada • Mexico • Singapore • Spain • United Kingdom • United States

Credits and permissions can be found on page 215
and should be considered an extension of the copyright page.

Schirmer is an imprint of Wadsworth,
a division of Thomson Learning, Inc.
Thomson Learning™ is a trademark
used herein under license.

Book design by Charles B. Hames

Library of Congress Catalog Number: 98-45504

Printed in the United States of America

Printing Number
2 3 4 5 6 7 8 9 10

LIBRARY OF CONGRESS CATALOGING-IN-PUBLICATION DATA

Duckworth, William.
20/20 : 20 new sounds of the 20th century / by William Duckworth.
p. cm.
Includes biobliographical references and index.
ISBN 0-02-864864-1
1. Music—20th century—History and criticism.
2. Musical analysis. I. Title. II. Title: Twenty/twenty.
ML197.D84 1999
780' .9'04'dc21   98-45504

CIP
MN

This paper meets the requirements of ANSI/NISO Z.39.48-1992 (Permanence of Paper).

for Nora

CONTENTS

Contents

Contents

Contents

Introduction

I've heard it said that when Western classical music was first introduced into the Asian subcontinent the listeners there were mystified. They thought it all sounded alike. I don't know if that's true, but the story seems to be a good analogy for the state many of us find ourselves in today, particularly when it comes to the concert music of our own century. While it may not all sound alike, it can certainly appear confusing, sometimes thorny, and generally difficult to get a handle on. Under the circumstances, who can blame today's listeners for retreating to the security of Beethoven and Tchaikovsky? At least with the classics you know what you're going to get. But is this really where listeners want to be today, holed up and dug in behind some imaginary Maginot Line for music? Defending the nineteenth century against the advancing twenty-first? The twentieth century is over, after all, and we're still, in some instances, questioning music written fifty and even a hundred years ago.

Part of the problem listeners face today is that there's no such thing anymore as *The World's Twenty-Five All-Time Favorite Melodies*, or favorite anything else for that matter, that everyone can more-or-less agree upon, dutifully go off to hear, and use as a yardstick against anything new. Although you may occasionally catch somebody on television trying to sell the latest spin on the idea, the truth of the matter is that the various streams of music that flow through our lives now move through a delta, not the deep, sure, stylistic channels they occupied prior to this century. Today, something new (different, strange) is always happening. Overlapping of styles is common. The musical history of this century, in fact, is a continuing saga of each new style being quickly rejected, assimilated, or transcended by the next. And this is equally true whether we're talking about jazz or rock or the avant-garde. So as listeners of today, no matter how astute, we are constantly being confronted by a kaleidoscope of musical sounds and genres, most of them unfamiliar, that are always changing, always evolving into something else, just when we think we're beginning to understand it. Things are at a point now where the two questions I'm asked most frequently as a composer, from audiences interested in hearing more new music, are *Where do I begin?* and *Where do I go now?* Odd questions to be discussing, if you think about it, considering the topic is a brief, hundred-year period of recent and living history.

By contrast and in our own defense, styles of music in previous centuries did not shift courses so quickly or so easily. Sure, there were variations and embellishments. And most styles grow and change as they mature. But the generally understood principles of how music was supposed to be written during the three hundred years prior to 1900 tended to stay relatively in place for decades, if not centuries, at a time. Look at the textbook dates for the Baroque (1600–1750), Classic (1750–1820), and Romantic (1820–1900) periods of music. Together, they define classical music in most people's minds. Think about that. This is THE three-hundred-year history of Western European art music, defined by only three broad styles. And if we leave Western Europe, we find styles that are relatively unchanged for thousands of years, such as *raga* in India, and *gagaku* in Japan. Twentieth-century Western music, on the other hand, is loaded with isms—primitivism, serialism, minimalism, and neo-Romanticism, to name but a few. We need a road map just to know where to begin. And if we find something we like—a place to begin—we need to know where to go next. But in a delta, unfortunately—particularly the new music delta we occupy now—the streets aren't laid out in a grid, and there aren't many road signs to point the way.

Maybe that's what this book will become for some: a way to begin, an introduction, a guided tour through the sounds of the classical music of our own time. For others, it may encourage a next step, a way to explore beyond the music they already know and love. For me, it's about making this music, these sounds, come alive for new listeners. I used to joke that the *sound* of new music was one of the best kept secrets of the twentieth century. Unfortunately, things haven't changed much in the twenty years since I first said it. So to the extent that I can, I'd like to give away as many of these secrets as possible. To show why this music is beautiful, in ways that everyone will understand.

As soon as I hit upon the idea of a book focusing on twenty sounds of the twentieth century, the big question for me suddenly became *Which twenty?* I had my favorites, of course. I made a list. But that seemed too shortsighted. Everybody, after all, has a bias. If I really wanted to write a book about twentieth-century classical music—a somewhat diaphanous genre, to say the least—in a way that would make it come alive and take on meaning, I felt I needed to have a better idea of what other people might feel about which twenty were the right ones. So I did a poll. Actually, I asked a few of my friends (fellow composers, men and women, not all Americans) if they would each make their own list; I wanted to compare theirs with mine. But I didn't phrase the question in the way you might expect. Instead of wanting to know which pieces my friends thought were significant and worthy, I asked which pieces mattered most to them personally. Which ones had really made a difference in their lives. What I found was that we are, in fact, living in a musical delta. Our lists overlapped on fewer than one-third of the works. We disagreed, sometimes strongly, if not strangely, on fully two-thirds. Outside of a few "masterpieces" like *The Rite of Spring,* there was no general consensus, even among friends.

While my poll wasn't very scientific, it did produce the results I expected. As I saw it, I now had a working list that put the *sound* of the music ahead of everything else. After all, what could possibly be *moving* and *meaningful* about music, except the sound of it? I've included what I took to calling the Long List in Appendix A. Listeners on the lookout for new works would do well to begin their search there.

I reduced the Long List to a final group of twenty by applying the following criteria: first, each of the pieces I selected had to be meaningful to me personally. My reasoning was that if I didn't believe in it—if the music hadn't made a difference in my life—I would never be able to convince other people of its worth and beauty. Second, I decided to include only pieces that have been performed steadily and widely since they were written. It only makes sense to discuss music a lot of people have already heard, or at least heard about. Third, I decided to focus on pieces that are not only available on compact disc, but that have a fifty/fifty chance of actually being found at the local mall. I thought it was important to deal with music that, in some sense at least, was, and is, both popular and available. Fourth, and this is more nebulous and subjective, I wanted to talk about music that I thought would be around for a while—music by the Bachs and Beethovens of our time, if you will.

As we begin, one last point deserves reemphasis. This book is about sound. Musical sound. The sounds of our time. The more you listen to the music, the more sense everything will make. Go toward the sounds that you like. Explore from there.

Finally, in order to really understand the importance of all these perhaps unfamiliar names and pieces, we need to build a grid in our minds, a place to store and sort all the various bits of information. A way of telling what's significant, and what's not. And since that's the case, what better way to begin than with the age-old game of Twenty Questions, the point of which, after all, is to obtain the information one wants in as little time as possible.

Twenty Questions about New Music

1. How do I begin to try to understand new music?

Begin with the sound. No matter what type of music you enjoy today, your love for it almost certainly started with the sound. So a good way to begin exploring new sounds is to let your ear be your guide. Listen to the music you read about here; most of it is widely available in both libraries and record stores. Play it first, even before you read anything. And from what you hear, choose something that appeals to you and begin there. Exploring by ear, after all, is what new music is all about. Most experimental composers, particularly those of the avant-garde, are in love with sound, all kinds of it. They use sound in both traditional and nontraditional ways; the variety is enormous. So allowing your ear to guide you to sounds that intrigue you is a valid way to begin.

2. How can I use this book to help me?

The traditional way to begin, or course, is chronologically, reading the book from cover to cover, and listening to as many of the pieces as you can. With this method, you'll develop an understanding of the history of this music, and how its various styles all fit together. Also, by approaching it this way, you'll hear the music in the order it was written, new sound after new sound. My preference, however, is still to let your ear be your guide, not only through this book, but beyond, as well. Select the pieces and composers that you like and start there, letting each new experience lead you to the next. But no matter which method you decide to use, however, remember as you begin that all music—regardless of where it's from, or what it sounds like—is made from six basic elements. It's the relative weighing and balancing of these fundamental components—always an individual effort—that allows composers, even those working within the same style, to sound so different from each other. These basic ingredients are melody, rhythm, harmony, timbre, texture, and form; and it is through these that we will explore what's new in the music of our time.

3. Why does this new music sound so different from the music of the past?

This question has been asked hundreds of times over the years; it's not new to the twentieth century. The answer, however, is never the same. For us, today, there are several reasons why we may still find the music of this century unfamiliar. First, since the late 1800s, composers have been combining and balancing the basic elements of musical sound in ways they had not tried before. Suddenly, or so it seemed, rhythm, timbre, and texture sometimes became more important than harmony and melody. That, of course, changed the sound of things rather quickly. Another reason, and one more difficult to explain, is that the working definition of music also changed radically, and often, during the century. Not only did composers focus on elements beyond melody and harmony, they also began to incorporate a multitude of new *sounds* into their music; running the gamut from unusual orchestral instruments, to electronic and computer sounds, to chance-produced noises, to absolute silence (four minutes and thirty-three seconds of it by John Cage, to mention the most famous example). Cage even wrote pieces with no beginnings, middles, or ends, and pieces in which the only sounds produced were environmental and unintentional. By that point in the century, the question *Is THAT music?* had grown pretty loud.

4. How can I begin to make sense out of something so new and different?

Keep in mind that everybody's music was new at one time or another. And new almost always sounds *different,* if not strange; at least it has in this century. If it doesn't sound strange at first, it's probably not new. Music that sounds immediately familiar builds on the past, it doesn't break with it. There's nothing wrong with that, of course. A whole world of highly crafted, quasi-tonal music was written during the century, much of it beautiful, too. Ultimately, however, the question is not whether some unknown piece of music sounds pleasant or not, but whether you're willing, as a listener, to suspend judgment, and approach the music with an open mind. And whether, once you've done that, it has something in it that keeps you listening. That's the key to enjoying unfamiliar music. You don't have to like what you hear, in the same way that you probably don't like every new movie you see. Also, keep in mind that the sound of some experimental music can be difficult, even for people who know its context. On first hearing, and without a background, some of it can seem impossible. If you find yourself in one of those places, just remember that there are many different styles to choose from. And that almost no one likes them all.

5. Why should I listen to music I may not like?

Maybe you shouldn't, but how do you know you won't like it if you've never heard it? Those noisy, atonal, arrhythmic, and nonmelodic sounds many people associate with today's music are, in reality, only a fraction of the many varieties of musical sounds that have been created over the century. New music is a multicolored mosaic of sounds. There's always a new one you haven't heard. Some of it is influenced by classical techniques; others of it have roots in rock, world music, or jazz. It also helps to remember that the composers of the twentieth century were often mavericks, working in relative isolation, cultivating their own unique set of sounds. No two of them sound alike, and the differences between them can be enormous. If you're willing to explore a bit, you won't have much trouble finding something that you'll like.

6. Did classical music give listeners of the previous century this much trouble?

Yes, although the experimentation in our century has been greater than in most. But consider the following comments from composers, reviewers and essayists of the nineteenth century[1]:

> Beethoven always sounds to me like the upsetting of bags of nails
>
> *John Ruskin (letter to John Brown), 1881*

> I played over the music of that scoundrel Brahms. What a giftless bastard!
>
> *Tchaikovsky's Diary, 1886*

> Chopin increasingly effects the crudest modulations. Cunning must be the connoisseur, indeed, who, while listening to his music, can form the slightest idea when wrong notes are played.
>
> **The Athenaeum**, *London, 1845*

> Tchaikovsky's First Piano Concerto, like the first pancake, is a flop.
>
> **Novoye Vremya**, *St. Petersburg, Russia, 1875*

> [Wagner] produces the same effect upon you, and gives you the same pain, as if a hundred needles should enter your ear at once.
>
> **Musical Times**, *Boston, 1861*

A hundred needles in the ear? That seems a bit excessive, even for Wagner, but it does illustrate how the new is often misunderstood. Today, we may find it difficult to believe that anyone could have felt that way about the music of Chopin and Brahms. But by the same token, future listeners may find our reactions to today's experimental music equally puzzling. That's not so difficult to believe if you consider that even now, less than a hundred years later, many listeners have trouble understanding why Stravinsky's *The Rite of Spring* caused a riot at its premiere. We hear the piece today and think, *What was the big deal?*

---

1. From Nicolas Slonimsky's *Lexicon of Musical Invective* (University of Washington Press, 2d ed., 1975). Subtitling it "Critical Assaults on Composers Since Beethoven's Time," Slonimsky has included an "Invecticon" index of "vituperative, pejorative and deprecatory words and phrases." If you enjoy seeing history prove the critics wrong, you'll love this book.

7. What do the terms "new," "experimental," and "contemporary" actually mean?

These are the broad, all-encompassing labels that were applied, at various times, to particular segments of twentieth-century music. When they first appeared, each label had a specific meaning, and referred to music that had broken with the past in some significant way. But as the century progressed and newer styles appeared, these broad terms began to lose their significance for the average listener. The term *new music*, for instance, has been used in too many different ways during the century. The problem is that when someone refers to *new music* today, too many conflicting images can come to mind. *Experimental music* is another nebulous term, and one that is often used synonymously with *new music*. Lately, however, the meaning of this label has become even more confused. Now if you tell someone you listen to experimental music, they may think you mean the outer edges of rock. The exclusive property of classical music until the 1980s, the terms *experimental* and *contemporary* are now being used as synonyms for alternative rock.

8. What is the avant-garde?

Avant-garde is a French military term. It means the people in front, the ones that venture into enemy territory first. That's also just about what it meant when it was applied, worldwide, to the arts in the 1960s. The avant-garde were the people doing the experiments, and pushing the definition of art as far as they could. In America, these were musicians like John Cage, Robert Ashley, Pauline Oliveros, and Alvin Lucier. Today, unfortunately, the term is slowly growing obscure. As things stand now, *avant-garde* can be used synonymously with *experimental*, while *experimental* is often a substitute for *contemporary*, unless, of course, we're talking about *alternative rock*. Is it any wonder that today's music can seem so confusing?

The basic problem with labels is that they are extremely contextual. Out of time and place, and without background, they don't really tell us anything. Perhaps the best all-encompassing term for the music of today, and the one that may continue to mean something in the next century, is *twentieth-century music*. At its broadest, it means all of the music written during the past one hundred years. Everything. As applied to the classical music of the century, it accepts everybody, from the most conservative to the most radical and avant-garde.

9. How many different styles of twentieth-century music are there?

I don't know. And I don't know anyone who does anymore, either. But here are the ones I can think of:

Ambient	Futurism	Noise Music
Barbarism	Impressionism	Orientalism
Chance Music	Indeterminacy	Polytonalism
Computer Music	Maximalism	Postminimalism
Dadaism	Microtonalism	Primitivism
Electronica	Minimalism	Serialism
Electronic Music	Musique concrète	Structuralism
Exoticism	Nationalism	Totalism
Expressionism	Neo-Classicism	
Fluxus	Neo-Romanticism	

10. How can I possibly keep all of these "isms" straight?

The best answer, probably, is don't try; the sound is more important than the label. Besides, some of these "isms" don't seem as accurate or important as they once did. Labels always get applied after the fact. Instead, think about how you learned to love and enjoy what you listen to now. Probably, you found a sound that intrigued you, stayed with it, learned a few names, and explored from there. Slowly—and enjoyably, no doubt—you accumulated a fairly sizable body of knowledge. Over the years, you may have repeated this pattern several times. Many people today know and appreciate five or six different styles. New music should be learned the same way. Each new piece you find takes you to something else. Before you know it, a discriminating appreciation has developed, just as it did with whatever you know and like now.

11. Why does one century contain so many different styles of music?

Cars, planes, radios, televisions, satellites, computers—the inventions of the century—all radically changed how music was disseminated. Once, it took years for a new style of music to be heard throughout Europe. Today, that happens routinely in a matter of days and weeks. The reason new styles occur faster now is not only because communications move more quickly, but also because everything now has at least the potential of influencing everything else. With a few remote exceptions, the music of the world is now instantly available to all.

12. Why does the music of the twentieth century seem so hectic, in comparison with music of the past?

Music, like all the arts, reflects the values and activities of the culture from which it comes. That's one of the reasons we study the arts—to learn what we can about people from another time and place. The rhythms of today's music, for instance, sound different from those of the past. This is true in both our music and our daily lives. If twentieth-century music tends to sounds hectic, or noisy—or even uncertain, at times, as to its proper direction among so many possibilities—it is because the century itself has been hectic, and noisy—and sometimes out of control. The hectic pace, glittering variety, and constant distractions of our daily lives are mirrored in our arts.

13. Why do some pieces of experimental music continue for such long lengths of time?

It has to do with how the music is constructed, and where the attention is drawn. Think of the difference between a one-hour drama and a thirty-minute sitcom. With a longer time frame, plots can become more intricate and characters more fully drawn. As a result, classical pieces of music are generally longer than most popular ones. Beyond that, some of this century's composers have become fixated on time, the way others have been fascinated with sound. Their experiments with time have resulted in pieces of enormous length, ones that can take days or even weeks to perform. This play on time came as a reaction to the accelerated pace of twentieth-century life.

14. Where is the line between music and noise?

There is none today; it's blurred beyond belief. And that is just as true for popular music as it is for experimental. During the century, noise has been used to make beautiful music. Some music, on the other hand, definitely sounds like noise. The line, if there is one, is different, and personal, for each listener. For composers, it is centered somewhere in intent: What is the composer trying to do? What is the purpose of the noise? Why is the composer using these particular sounds? When the context of a noise piece is better understood, the "noise" it contains may take on a new meaning, and be heard in a different way.

15. What is modern music trying to say?

Modern music is not trying to say anything. Instead, it is a reflection of life—the one we are living. Taken as a whole, twentieth-century music is an aural portrait of the century. There is no secret message in this music that only the initiated can understand. This music, like all other music, contains the feelings, tensions, and aspirations of the times. Modern music is a reflection of us, of who we are, just as classical music reflects life in a different time and place. To paraphrase Marshall McLuhan, the music itself is the message, from us to future generations. In its own unique way, twentieth-century music will help to tell them who we were.

16. Why does some modern music sound so easy to make?

Just because music doesn't have a melody, or a pulse, or harmony you can recognize, doesn't mean it's easier to compose. Experimental music is neither easier nor more difficult to write than other kinds, including the most traditional and conservative. Whether composers use extended classical techniques, full of melodies and steady beats, or use noise, computers, and tape recorders to make their music, in the end, the effort is the same. As the composers of this century began to abandon traditional methods and turn their attention in other directions, the music they created, at least for some listeners, seemed to have no context. It sounded out of control, and sometimes even gave listeners the feeling that anything goes. And while occasionally that has been true, more often it has not. So the next time you hear music that you think could have been written by anyone, consider, first, that your reaction may be the result of a conflict between the composer's aims and your expectations. Try, instead, to understand why the composer *chose* to use these particular sounds in this particular way. The more difficult question, and one everyone must answer for him- or herself, is whether music that sounds random is, in some way, faking it. Occasionally the answer is yes; more often it is no.

17. How do I know what is good?

You don't, at least not when you first begin. This is particularly true when dealing with twentieth-century music, and the panoply of styles its composers have produced. The only way we can begin to make these kinds of discriminations is by having a response to something. It's from these initial reactions, and the knowledge acquired around them, that we begin to develop a sense of appreciation, and an "ear" for what is good. In the meantime, find something you like and go from there.

18. What is the difference between art and entertainment in twentieth-century music?

The difference is one of depth and intent. Think about the novels you've read. Some are amusing; others have a more lasting value that deals with important human issues in a sensitive and intelligent way. Books of this type offer deep exposure to questions on emotional and intellectual levels. Consider, for instance, Dostoyevsky's *Crime and Punishment*, and how the novel explores the question of guilt. You won't find that depth of feeling and understanding in the average drugstore detective novel, however entertaining it may be. Art, to be art, must go beyond mere amusement; it's the difference between a southern belle in a Harlequin romance and Tolstoy's Anna Karenina. A work of art, on the other hand, is generally thought to offer a means of getting closer to our deeper feelings. Art plays on our emotions, the most unexamined aspect of experience. While we live most of our lives somewhere between the physical and intellectual modes of existence, it is only through emotional perception that we can get a perspective on feeling. Art, it is generally agreed, has the potential to put us in touch with ourselves. And if art is challenging to the senses, as much of contemporary art is, it pushes and extends our perceptual boundaries. This is not the same as entertainment.

19. Is this the new classical music of the future?

It's too soon to say. Listening to the music of today, we lack the perspective of time, and our opinions may, or may not, withstand the judgments of history. We don't know what listeners of the future will want to hear. And while twentieth-century music is the rightful heir and successor to the European classical tradition, it is, in some instances, a very different kind of music from the music of that tradition's previous three hundred years. Not only have the forms of music changed, but even the instruments themselves. And the aesthetics, in some cases, have changed so radically, that over the course of time twentieth-century music may become a genre all its own.

20. Where do I go from here?

The best way to learn about new music is to keep listening; there is always something new to hear. It is hoped that this book will give you some background and a place to begin. Use these pieces as starting points from which to branch out to other new sounds. Then, begin looking for live concerts in your area. Also, check your local record stores. The large chains frequently have fairly good selections of twentieth-century music; the smaller ones often specialize in things that may intrigue you. They will all be glad to order anything you might want. Beyond that, check the program guide of your local NPR station. Many stations broadcast nationally syndicated programs like Stephen Hill's *Music from the Hearts of Space* and John Schaefer's *New Sounds*. In the twenty-first century, the place to find new music will be the worldwide web. Many composers already have home pages, and some have begun to put up sounds. New music won't be as difficult to locate in the next century as it was, at times, during ours.

1

Prelude to the Afternoon of a Faun

CLAUDE DEBUSSY

1894

Debussy's *Prelude to the Afternoon of a Faun*, his most celebrated work, was written when he was thirty-three years old. First performed in Paris on December 22, 1894, it startled the listeners of the time with its "luminescent orchestral color" and "breathtaking sensuality." Despite its unfamiliar sound, it met with such immediate success that it had to be played again that same evening as an encore. The next season it was heard twice more, appearing on two separate series in Paris late in the fall. Within a few years, Debussy's *Prelude* was being played by what seemed to be every orchestra in Europe. The first chance Americans had to hear it was in Boston in 1902. That was a year before Ferruccio Busoni conducted it in Berlin, and several years before Arturo Toscanini led it in Turin and Richard Strauss performed it in Vienna. Debussy, a reluctant conductor of average abilities, was eventually persuaded by the *Prelude*'s ever-increasing success and his own growing fame to conduct it in various places throughout Europe, including the 1913 opening of the new Théâtre des Champs Elysées. That came only a year after the famed Ballet Russes, Sergei Diaghilev's Russian ballet—in Paris yearly since 1909—staged the *Prelude*, choreographed and danced by the legendary dancer Vaslav Nijinsky.

Claude Debussy. *Corbis-Bettmann*

What makes a piece of music burst onto the musical scene, calling attention to itself and disrupting the status quo, as this one obviously did? The reasons, always different of course, are subtle and elusive. In Debussy's case, the clues lie in the words *luminescent color* and *breathtaking sensuality*, two phrases I found in Richard Langham

Smith's translation of Debussy's critical writings. But what did luminescent color sound like a hundred years ago? And what was breathtakingly sensual about a piece of music based on an eighteen-year-old poem?

To answer the second question first, the important thing to remember about Debussy's *Prelude to the Afternoon of a Faun* is that the faun in question is not a baby deer. Far from it. For Stéphane Mallarmé, the Symbolist poet whose *Afternoon of a Faun* inspired Debussy to write his orchestra piece, the faun is a shadowy half-man, half-beast figure, complete with hoofs and horns. At the beginning of Mallarmé's poem the faun lies asleep, warming in the afternoon sun, and dreaming lascivious dreams of the nymphs he is obsessed with. His successes at luring nymphs with his flute float by in his mind. Mallarmé is intentionally vague about what actually happens, and even about the order in which things occur, but the atmosphere the poem evokes is overflowing with sensual impressions. This particular afternoon the faun, no longer young, dreams, or sees, two nymphs who "*lie sleeping, tangled in their accidental arms.*" He goes on: "*Alone; I seize them, not untangling them, and run.*" His plan is to spend the day in sensual pleasure, of which, he recalls, "*They drink, quivering like lightning, . . . Two in one instant forgoing innocence.*" But just as suddenly their images vanish, and the faun, uncertain of what has happened, sinks back into sleep. You can imagine the stir this caused when it was published in 1876, in a slim, elegantly bound volume, complete with a line-drawing of the nymphs by Edouard Manet.

Debussy on Music

Music is a mysterious mathematical process whose elements are a part of Infinity. It is allied to the movement of the waters, to the play of curves described by the changing breezes. Nothing is more musical than a sunset!

Musica, 1903

It seems to me that although music was never meant to confine itself solely to the world of dreams, it doesn't gain anything by concerning itself too much with everyday life. It is weakened by trying to be too human, for its primary essence is mystery.

Gil Blas, 1903

I myself love music passionately, and through my love I have forced myself to break free from certain sterile traditions with which it is encumbered. It is a free art, a wellspring, an art of the open air, an art comparable to the elements—the wind, the sea, and the sky!

interview in Excelsior, 1911

By its very nature music is more likely to contain something of the magical than any other art.

SIM, 1913

What Debussy has done musically is capture the unspoken moods of Mallarmé's poem in sound. His interest lies in the sensual impressions created by the words, not in depicting the actual events of the poem. The program notes for the Paris premiere (certainly approved by Debussy, if not written by him) describe the *Prelude* as "successive scenes of the faun's desires and dreams in the heat of the afternoon." In a letter to an influential French critic, Debussy suggested that his music might be fragments of the faun's dream still lingering in the flute. The Viennese critic Ernst Decsey, when he first heard the *Prelude*, said Debussy had created a scene of pagan sensuality. Mallarmé, who was delighted, said, "I was not expecting anything of this kind!"

The way Debussy evokes such pagan scenes musically is by treating melody, harmony, and rhythm in new and completely unexpected ways. His melodies, sounding almost improvised, float in the air, changing like clouds, not going any place in particular. His chords, some of five and six different pitches, create exotic clouds of sound that move in parallel motion with the melody more often than they do in harmonically logical progressions toward classical cadences. And his rhythms are so fluctuating and subtle that some critics of the time insisted that *Prelude to the Afternoon of a Faun* had no rhythm at all. The result is music that shimmers like shadows.

Still, it's one thing to begin with a sexy poem, quite another to create orchestral music that startles and delights an audience. To understand how a Frenchman in his early thirties, with a traditional musical education from the Paris Conservatory, could discover such a spectacular new way to compose music, we must begin ten years earlier, in 1884. That was the year, fresh from the Conservatory, that Debussy won the Prix de Rome, a prize that sent him to Italy for several years to compose. He went, as he said, "full of the Wagnerian madness," meaning that he was caught up in the current wave of Wagner-worship then sweeping Europe; he returned, two years later, with music the evaluation committee of the Paris Académie de Beaux-Arts described as "vague impressionism," something they warned Debussy to "be on his guard against." What they meant was that he went too far in the direction of "exaggerated musical color," and not far enough toward remembering the importance of "precise construction" and "purity of form." Debussy, some years later, said he hated that kind of classical development, and preferred that his music be free of those silly obsessions and sterile traditions. He also said he wanted his music to emerge from "the mysterious affinity between Nature and the Imagination."

Debussy on Wagner

At this time [1885] I was Wagnerian to the point of forgetting the most fundamental good manners.

Gil Blas, 1903

Wagner . . . was a beautiful sunset that has been mistaken for a sunrise.

Mercure de France, 1903

An old friend of mine, M. Croche (who died recently), used to call the *Ring* the "Who's Who of the Gods."

Les Annales Politiques et Litteraires, 1913

I am no longer an adversary of Wagner. Wagner is a genius, but geniuses can make mistakes. Wagner pronounced himself in favor of the laws of harmony. I am for freedom.

statement to an Austrian journalist, 1910

In the years between his return to Paris in 1887 and his writing of the *Prelude*, which he began five years later, several events took place that significantly altered Debussy's musical thinking. One was his two trips to Germany in 1888 and again the next year, to hear Richard Wagner's music in the theater (some said shrine) Wagner had managed to have built to his specifications in the town of Bayreuth, a theater dedicated solely to performances of his own operas. The other was the Paris World Exhibition of 1889, for which, among other things, the Eiffel Tower was built. It was there that Debussy came into contact with the music of Africa and Asia.

Wagnermania swept the musical world of late-nineteenth-century Europe. By the 1870s Wagner, through the sheer quality and quantity of his music, combined with his great promotional skills and enormous desire for acclaim, overshadowed all other living composers. It gives us some inkling of what his stature must have been, to realize that performances of his operas are still taking place in his theater in Bayreuth today, more than a century after his death, and that people are still flocking there to hear them. So for young European composers of the time there were really only two creative avenues available. One was the more conservative and traditional route through Brahms, with his symphonies and sonatas. The other was the more adventuresome and groundbreaking path through Wagner, and his new operatic form he called the *music drama*. To Wagner, drama and music were not only inseparable, they had to actively support each other, as well. In his new music dramas, particularly his four-opera cycle, *The Ring of the Nibelung*, people, things, and even ideas have their own phrase of music, or *leitmotif*, with which they are identified. This allows, among other things, for characters, objects, and emotions to be called to mind by the orchestra without actually being mentioned or appearing on stage. And this, in turn, allows Wagner to create a psychological web of relationships, musical and otherwise, and to manipulate it in all manner of ways. Meanwhile, the music, which is almost continuous melody (never ending, some say), stretches to the limit the Romantic composer's desire fully to explore the furthest recesses of chromaticism without actually abandoning classical tonality.

Debussy's artistic relationship to Wagner is complicated and seldom black or white. In his student days he wholeheartedly embraced Wagner, and continued to believe in him through his first visit to Bayreuth. But he soon came to believe that Wagner's success, as great as it was, was in creating complex musical formulas of use only to him. He also felt it was a mistake to insist, as Wagner had, that musical development—that is, how music grows and is controlled in time—should be responsible for supporting the dramatic action. And although it was a gradual process, Debussy finally came to believe that Wagner had "put the final period after the music of his time." What this realization did for Debussy was to free him, in some kind of final way, from his musical past—the weight of history, and the technical restraints. By the time he began the *Prelude to the Afternoon of a Faun* in 1892, his thoughts were turning toward creating music that would be uniquely French.

Debussy on Art

To believe that one can judge a work of art upon a first hearing is the strangest and most dangerous of delusions.

The Etude, 1914

Like Nature herself, Art changes: she moves in curved lines but always ends up exactly at the point where she began.

unpublished article, 1912

As a general rule, every time someone tries to complicate an art form or a sentiment, it is simply because they are unsure of what they want to say.

SIM, 1913

The other important event of this time for Debussy was the 1889 *Exposition Universelle*, as it was called in Paris. This early world's fair brought together musicians from many different nations, who played in simulated native villages, parks, and small booths around the city. Debussy went repeatedly to hear them, and was particularly drawn to the Javanese gamelan, an orchestra made up of tuned gongs and percussion.

He also heard two concerts of Russian music conducted by Rimsky-Korsakov, music seldom heard in Paris at the time. There, too, he heard strange new scales taken from folk music, exotic rhythms, and unusual chords unlike any he had been taught at the Conservatory. Gradually, he began to forge an alternative to his impasse with Wagner and the classical tradition. But Debussy, in incorporating these new ideas, didn't abandon the resources of his past. Instead, he became one of the first Western musicians to bring together a classical understanding of the music of Bach, Mozart, Beethoven, and Wagner with the age-old music of the Far East.

Technically, what Debussy succeeded in doing was weakening the hold that harmony and tonality have always had on classical music. He did this through a newfound freedom to use dissonant sounds and unfamiliar scales, and by violating some of the most basic *rules* of traditional counterpoint and harmony. While Debussy's melodies always predominate over rhythm and harmony, they seem only slightly related to classical melodies, which exhibit more defined shapes and clearer harmonic goals. Debussy's melodies, in comparison, sound vague and ambiguous. This is because he continually, or so it seems, changes the scale on which the melody is based, often using more than one type of scale within a single phrase, and certainly never basing a complete section on only one. Instead, he writes melodies made from chromatic scales with their complete lack of a tonal center; from whole-tone scales and the ambiguity created by their lack of half steps; from pentatonic scales with step-and-a-half gaps in them allowing any tone to be the fundamental; and from modal scales with the varying degrees of vagueness they supply. All of this, of course, is put at the service of melody, to keep it sounding forever fresh and vibrant, by rendering the tonic note, and thus the key center, always slightly uncertain.

Debussy on Composing

There is no Debussy school. I have no disciples; I am myself.

statement to an Austrian journalist, 1910

For many centuries we have been using the same sounds to express our innermost dreams, just as in writing we have been using the same words. There is very little difference. But when we realize that there are dozens of ways of writing or composing, there remain a hundred questions to be answered, and a further hundred posed by the answers themselves.

SIM, 1913

Who can know the secret of musical composition? The sound of the sea, the outline of a horizon, the wind in the leaves, the cry of a bird—these set off complex impressions in us. And suddenly, without the consent of anyone on this earth, one of these memories bursts forth, expressing itself in the language of music.

interview in **Excelsior***, 1911*

Although Debussy always maintains at least a sense of tonal center, he intentionally weakens the traditional relationships between chords, now seemingly chosen as much for color and sensuality as for their harmonic ability to point the emotional tension in the right direction and then release it. In a sense, Debussy frees his chords from their harmonic responsibility. By doing so, he is then able to allow some chords to last for entire phrases, creating an aura on which his melodies float. Others he moves in parallel with the melody, often in a series of parallel ninth chords (the first, or fundamental, third, fifth, seventh, and ninth pitches of the scale). And others he makes contribute to the expressiveness of various phrases, or reinforce the melodic cadences, without ever dispelling our sense of harmonic uncertainty. Paul Dukas, composer of the *Sorcerer's Apprentice* and sometime critic, wrote of the *Prelude* in 1903 that it is "located at the outer edges of the world of intelligible harmonies."

The problem today, of course, is that the sounds of the *Prelude to the Afternoon of a Faun* have become so familiar that many listeners underestimate their complexity and originality. The dazzling orchestral color that startled Debussy's listeners is all too well known, thanks to the literally hundreds of Hollywood movies of the thirties whose sound tracks imitated the style. But even though we're no longer startled by music we've known the entire century, we should not forget the fundamental importance of Debussy's *Prelude*. Debussy, more than any other single composer, opened the door to the sounds of the twentieth century. He was first to accept the music of other cultures into his own music, not as novelty, but in order to enliven it, a crossing of cultural boundaries that is commonplace today. And he was also the first to free musical sound, in all its manifestations, from the shackles of chord progressions, harmony, and form. And he did it while delighting not only his own audience, but audiences throughout the world for an entire century to come. Recollecting that someone once said that "the flute of the *Faun* brought new breath to the art of music," French composer and conductor Pierre Boulez added in 1958, "Modern music was awakened by the *Prelude to the Afternoon of a Faun*."

Debussy on Recordings

In a time like ours, when the genius of engineers has reached such undreamed of proportions, one can hear famous pieces of music as easily as one can buy a glass of beer. It only costs ten centimes, too, just like automatic weighing scales! Should we not fear this domestication of sound, this magic preserved in a disc that anyone can awaken at will? Will it not mean a diminution of the secret forces of art, which until now have been considered indestructible?

SIM, 1913

2

Maple Leaf Rag

SCOTT JOPLIN

1899

"Hello! ma baby, Hello! ma honey, Hello! ma ragtime gal." Say those lyrics from the 1890s aloud and listen to the rhythm. Rhythm is what ragtime is all about. Especially syncopation, a type of rhythm in which the accent falls where you least expect it. When Scott Joplin told a magazine writer in 1907 that his music was called ragtime "because it has such a ragged movement," rhythmic syncopation was what he was talking about. Say the lyrics again and you'll hear it, particularly if you say them fast and in tempo. Ragtime rhythm has a tension and an excitement that's somehow built in. A century later we feel the energy. Ragtime still makes us want to move.

But where did this new rhythm come from? In simplest terms, it came from the black subculture of the late nineteenth century. Joplin himself said in 1913 that ragtime (i.e., syncopated) music had been around ever since African Americans had arrived, but no one had paid any attention to it "until about twenty years ago." That would have meant 1893, the year of the World's Columbian Exposition in Chicago, where black ragtime pianists from all over America played, and where the sound of ragtime finally came to public attention. Scott Joplin was there, leading a band and playing cornet. So was John Philip Sousa, famed "March King" and director of the United States Marine Band.

Scott Joplin. *Corbis-Bettmann*

He, like most, was probably hearing ragtime for the first time. But not the last. Ragtime was just beginning. And whether in the form of songs, dances, ensemble pieces, or, most important, piano solos, it quickly became America's popular music, a position it held for twenty years. And of all this ragtime music, none was more popular, more performed, than Scott Joplin's *Maple Leaf Rag*.

It's hard to separate fact from fiction in the life of Scott Joplin. Partly it was the times, which were less obsessed with written documentation; partly it's the myth that has sprung up around him. Even the people actually involved—or their relatives, who swear that's just what they were told—tell different stories. What we do know is this. Scott Joplin was most likely born in late 1868, although even that's uncertain. He grew up in Texarkana, Texas, in a family where almost everyone played musical instruments. In his youth he played violin, the instrument his father played. Although his parents separated, his mother was able to buy him a piano by the time he was thirteen or fourteen. More importantly, he studied not only with local teachers, but with a German-immigrant musician, Julius Weiss, who recognized his talent and taught him for free in the formal European manner. It was through Weiss that Joplin gained an early understanding of European classical music.

Others on Ragtime

It was music of a kind I had never heard before. It was music that demanded physical response, patting of the feet, drumming of the fingers, or nodding of the head in time with the beat. The barbaric harmonies, the audacious resolutions, often consisting of an abrupt jump from one key to another, the intricate rhythms in which the accents fell in the most unexpected places, but in which the beat was never lost, produced a most curious effect.

songwriter and novelist James Weldon Johnson, 1912,

The President [Theodore Roosevelt] chose a partner and led the cakewalk down the long East Room, executing fancy buck and wing steps, while others in the party clapped "Juba."

New York World, 1901

While still a teenager, Joplin became a professional musician, singing in a quartet, playing piano, and teaching. After leaving Texarkana in the mid 1880s, he became a traveling musician, playing clubs, bars, and brothels up and down the Mississippi. We know for sure that he was in St. Louis in 1890, and Chicago in 1893. When the Chicago World's Fair ended in October, Joplin headed to St. Louis, and then to Sedalia, Missouri, a place he stayed for seven years. Sedalia was an ideal town for musicians looking for work. Ragtime expert Edward A. Berlin characterizes the Sedalia of the 1890s as a town of "pool halls, saloons, gambling dens, dance halls, and brothels." For Joplin, however, Sedalia meant not only employment, but friendships with other musicians, and a chance to attend college for a short time where, some say, he studied harmony and composition. By then, he was in his late twenties.

The Maple Leaf Club opened in Sedalia in 1898, with "Scott Joplin, the entertainer," as the business card read. Whether the name of the rag came from the club, or the other way around, isn't known for sure, but *Maple Leaf Rag* not only made Joplin's reputation, it gave him relative financial security. Joplin, it seems, instead of selling his music outright for twenty-five to fifty dollars, as was the practice of the time, brought his lawyer with him to negotiate a contract. Joplin received royalties. And *Maple Leaf Rag* sold hundreds of thousands of copies. It's still for sale today.

All these facts, however, don't yet tell us how the ragtime craze came about. To understand fully how music first played in saloons and brothels became suitable for social dancing at all levels of society, or why syncopation became the rhythm of choice for most young Americans, or how Scott Joplin, the son of a former slave, came to write the music most people heard as the sound of the new century, it's necessary to connect four aspects of late-nineteenth-century American musical life: the cakewalk, the march, sheet music, and the concert band. And to reflect for a moment on how these all came together at the turn of the century to create the phenomenon called ragtime.

Musically, what ragtime writers did was combine the style of the cakewalk, a plantation dance from the nineteenth century, with that of the European march. The cakewalk began as slaves parodying their white owners. By early in the new century, it was an international dance craze, thanks first to minstrel shows, then vaudeville, burlesque, and all-black musicals of the late 1890s. By that point, some of the bigger stars were touring Europe. Debussy, for instance, wrote his *Golliwogg's Cakewalk* in 1904, the dance being then all the rage in Paris. There were no particular steps associated with the cakewalk, just a parade-like walka-round in which couples strutted and pranced, each trying to outdo the other. The music, as you can imagine, was lively and syncopated, though not as much so as ragtime would soon become. From the cakewalk, ragtime writers took the idea of syncopation, which they then developed into an integral, identifying part of their music.

Scott Joplin on His Music

Syncopations are no indication of light or trashy music.

School of Ragtime, 1908

Notice! Don't play this piece fast. It is never right to play "rag-time" fast.

printed in the sheet music for **Leola,** 1905

"Joplin ragtime" is destroyed by careless or imperfect rendering, and very often good players lose the effect entirely, by playing too fast. They [rags] are harmonized with the supposition that each note will be played as it is written, as it takes this and also the proper time divisions to complete the sense intended.

School of Ragtime, 1908

I am a composer of ragtime music but I want it thoroughly understood that my opera "Treemonisha" is not ragtime.

New York Age, 1913

The nineteenth-century European march, on the other hand, was anything but syncopated. And as odd as it may seem today, march music of that era was thought to be as suitable an accompaniment for social dancing as it was for parade marching. Grand marches and polonaises supported opening processionals, while quicksteps accompanied the quadrilles and cotillions. From the march, ragtime writers took not only a steady, even accompaniment, but the overall musical shape. Marches, like other dances such as the polka and the two-step, consist of a series of three or more 16-measure units, or strains, most of which are repeated. Each strain is further divided into four 4-bar phrases, all very neat and even, easy to march (or dance) to. Ragtime writers simply took this musical shape as the form for their music. *Maple Leaf Rag* consists of four different 16-measure strains, grouped and repeated into a 9-strain pattern: AA BB A CC DD. It's not difficult to follow after a few hearings, particularly if you have a copy of the sheet music to look at.

Listen to *Maple Leaf Rag* and you'll see how musical elements from these two different cultures are put together. Rags are a reinterpretation of the march, with the feeling of the cakewalk. The right hand plays a highly syncopated *"Hello! ma baby"* melody; the left keeps a march-like, rock-steady, *oom-pah* pattern in the bass. Ragtime energy comes from the colliding, and simultaneous meshing, of these two contrasting ideas. Think about it this way: the right hand is playing in plain face; *the left hand is in italic.* While they're different from each other, they come together in a unique way to form something new. We can see the potential for interrelatedness when we consider that Joplin's first six published pieces consisted of two songs, two marches, a waltz, and a rag. *Maple Leaf Rag* was his seventh publication.

After hearing ragtime in Chicago in 1893, John Philip Sousa began almost immediately including band arrangements of rags on his concerts. Many people first heard ragtime in this version, since the Marine Band toured extensively from its base in Washington. By 1901, Sousa even had the band playing rags in the White House, Joplin's more than most. Three years later, parts for Joplin's rag were copied for the marching band, and in 1906 the band made its first recording of *Maple Leaf Rag.* It made a second in 1909. And even when people in Paris first heard ragtime, the odds are they also heard Sousa's band play it, since the Marine Band visited there several times early in the century. At the turn of the century, unlike today, concert bands were an integral part of musical life in both Europe and the United States.

Many people on both continents first experienced American ragtime in that form. You might say Sousa legitimized ragtime for a certain segment of society.

Debussy on John Philip Sousa

The king of American music is in town. By that I mean that M. J. P. Sousa and his band have come for a whole week to reveal to us the beauties of American music as it is performed in the best society. One really has to be exceedingly gifted to conduct this music. M. Sousa beats time in circles or tosses an imaginary salad or sweeps away some invisible dust. Or else he catches a butterfly that has flown out of a bass tuba!

Gil Blas, 1903

It's difficult today for most of us to realize how vital the publication of low-cost sheet music was to the dissemination of music in the first half of this century. Before records or radio, most people learned new music by buying the sheet music and playing it on the piano at home. The popular song industry thrived this way well into the 1950s. Joplin's publisher, John Stark, said that he had sold 500,000 copies of *Maple Leaf Rag* by 1909, and was selling 5,000 a month ten years later. This may be exaggerated somewhat, but even if it is, it's still extraordinary, and means that literally hundreds of thousands of homes across America had a copy of *Maple Leaf Rag* sitting on the parlor piano. Everybody who could play tried to play it. And perhaps the most intriguing thing about ragtime sheet music, from the perspective of today, is that this was the first time any African-American music was put down on paper in such a way that it could later be accurately reproduced. The music is there for anyone to study, then, now, or a hundred years in the future. The ragtime revival of the 1970s, for instance, could never have happened had there been no ragtime sheet music, or had it not accurately portrayed the sound of ragtime.

There's one other side to this story that has yet to be told. Scott Joplin always had ambitions beyond ragtime. He saw himself not only as an entertainer, but also as a composer of art music, doing for ragtime what Chopin had done for the mazurka. Stride pianist Willie "The Lion"

Smith recalled that Joplin's widow once showed him "Scott's cellar full of manuscripts," which he said included "modern things" and "classical pieces." When Joplin moved to New York in 1907, one possible reason was to try to realize his desire to work in both musical theater and opera. His first apartment was located in the theater district, a block away from the original Tin Pan Alley. And although his theatrical ambitions met with obstacles, Joplin still was able to both publish and produce his second opera, *Treemonisha*.

The Case Against Ragtime

The Black 400 and Maple Leaf clubs are a detriment to the morals of our people—affording a loafing place for many of our girls and boys, where they drink, play cards, dance, and we have been informed, carry on other immoral practices, too disgraceful to mention.

*an open letter from the Black ministers, **Sedalia Capital**, 1899*

Ragtime has dulled their taste for pure music just as intoxicants dull a drunkard's taste for pure water. Ragtime becomes a habit, and like all other habits, it is very difficult if not impossible for its victims to break away from it.

***Musical America**, 1912*

The counters of the music stores are loaded with this virulent poison which, in the form of a malarious epidemic, is finding its way into the homes and brains of the youth to such an extent as to arouse one's suspicions of their sanity.

***English Review**, 1913*

Scott Joplin died in New York in 1917, two weeks before the United States entered World War I. By the time the war ended, a new sound had replaced ragtime in the public's ear. That might have been the end of the story had it not been for several ragtime revivals, the biggest of which occurred in the 1970s around the movie *The Sting*. That was when the New York Public Library published almost all of Joplin's music in a two-volume set, when his records topped the charts, and when *Treemonisha* was not only seen in a properly staged, operahouse version, but even had a run on Broadway. Once again, Scott Joplin had become a household name in America, complete this time with a special Bicentennial Pulitzer Prize in 1976, and his picture on a United States postage stamp in 1983. Success had finally arrived, a little late, perhaps, but just as Joplin had said it would. As he told publisher Edward B. Marks, "When I'm dead twenty-five years, people are going to begin to recognize me."

On Ragtime's Place in History

Those who play Joplin's music carefully will find a suggestion of profound thought in it. . . . [It appeals] to the cultured as well as the amateur, and will bear repetition without number, growing more popular with age.

American Musician and Art Journal, 1907

Of the character of "rag-time" there can be no doubt—it is absolutely characteristic of its inventors—from nowhere but the United States could such music have sprung. . . . Here, perhaps, then, for those who have ears to hear are the seeds from which a national art may ultimately spring.

Times, London, 1913

[Joplin's] rags can only be described as elegant, varied, often subtle, and as sharply incised as a cameo. They are the precise American equivalent, in terms of a native style of dance music, of minuets by Mozart, mazurkas by Chopin, or waltzes by Brahms.

*Musicologist H. Wiley Hitchcock, **Stereo Review**, 1971*

For several weeks over the past year, the entire list of "Best Sellers" has been comprised of nothing but the works of Scott Joplin, making him the classical phenomenon of the decade.

***Record World**, 1974*

3

The Rite of Spring

IGOR STRAVINSKY

1913

Why did Igor Stravinsky's ballet score *The Rite of Spring* (*La sacre du printemps*), written for the impresario Serge Diaghilev's famed Ballet Russes, and premiered in Paris at the grand opening of the Théâtre des Champs-Elysées in the spring of 1913, create a riot? No one expected it, least of all Stravinsky. His two earlier ballet scores, *The Firebird* (1910) and *Petrushka* (1911), both written for the Ballet Russes, and premiered during its yearly visits to Paris, had met with great critical and popular success, and Stravinsky, already famous, had every reason to believe this new ballet would be his crowning achievement. The dress rehearsal the night before, attended by Debussy and Ravel, as well as by most of the Paris press and a number of artists, had given no hint of what was in store. Everyone applauded and went home. But at the premiere, this thirty-five-minute work by the thirty-year-old Stravinsky produced some of the most disruptive and violent reactions from the audience the musical world has ever seen.

Stravinsky begins the ballet with a solo by the bassoon, played high in its range: soft . . . delicate . . . haunting. Almost immediately, the laughter, whistling, and foot stomping began. Within minutes, the counter-demonstrations sprang up. When the orchestra started repeating the

Igor Stravinsky. *Corbis-Bettmann*

same massive, bitonal chord, built on keys a second apart, over and over—some 280 times before the piece ended—and the dancers, dressed as American Indians (then considered the most exotic culture on earth by Europeans) began stomping in some prehistoric tribal circle, the situation dissolved into chaos. Neither the dancers nor the audience could hear the music. The atmosphere quickly grew so charged that Stravinsky left his seat in the fourth row and stood backstage with Vaslav Nijinsky, the famous dancer and, in this case, choreographer, who, according to Stravinsky, was threatening to rush on stage and start his own riot. Diaghelev had the house lights flashed on and off, but to no effect. When it was over, and the chosen one had danced herself to death to music that jerked and leaped in combinations of irregular meters and rhythms never before imagined, much less heard, the commotion spread to the street, where car horns blared and fistfights are said to have erupted.

Today, it's difficult for us to understand what all the fuss was about. So much controversial music has been written, and the boundaries of music have been stretched so far beyond where they were in 1913, that it is impossible for us to hear *The Rite of Spring* in any way resembling what the original audience would have heard. Today, it can sound almost tame. André Boucourechliev, the author of *Stravinsky*, suggests the original violence may have started because these unfamiliar, brutal, and repetitive sounds were presented within a musical framework that was still, in 1913, understandable enough to be taken seriously, judged, and rejected by the Paris public. He also said Diaghilev may have had a hand in provoking the incident, giving away tickets with the instructions "to applaud the work at all costs." Others say that the scandal, if there was one, has been blown out of all proportion to reality. But what everyone agrees with is that the premiere, on May 29, 1913, of Igor Stravinsky's *The Rite of Spring*, more than any other single event, defines the beginning of modern music.

Although Stravinsky came from a musical family, he didn't plan to be a composer until he was almost twenty. His father was a leading bass singer with the Imperial Opera in St. Petersburg, so it was natural for the young Stravinsky to began piano lessons when he was nine. He heard his first orchestra music—Glinka's *A Life for the Tsar*—with his mother shortly thereafter. He once caught a glimpse of Tchaikovsky. But he studied law at the University of St. Petersburg; it seems his parents wanted him to become a government lawyer, a safe job before the revolution. So it was only in the summer of 1903, within two years of leaving the university, that Stravinsky visited Nikolai Rimsky-Korsakov, the father of a fellow student and leading composer of the Russian nationalist school, about the possibility of composition lessons. The lessons, which began that autumn, continued for three years. By that point, Stravinsky had left the university and was married.

Although the violent reaction evoked by the premiere was unexpected, a few people did realize that *The Rite of Spring* was fundamentally different from either *The Firebird* or *Petrushka*. The previous summer, Stravinsky had played a two-piano version of his new score at the home of Louis Laloy, with Debussy as the second pianist. Laloy later said, "We were dumbfrounded, thunderstruck as though by a hurricane from the remote past, which had seized our lives by the roots." In a letter written on the day of the premiere, Debussy himself described the experience as an "extraordinary savage affair," and went on to add, "You might call it primitive with every modern convenience." And Pierre Monteux, the conductor of the orchestra that first night, said Stravinsky had played a solo piano version for him and Diaghilev, and that "before he got very far I was convinced he was raving mad."

But what is this infamous piece, *The Rite of Spring*, all about? How does it actually sound? It is written in two large sections: *The Adoration of the Earth* and *The Sacrifice*. Stravinsky said the idea came to him in 1910 in St. Petersburg as he was finishing *The Firebird*. He continues, "I had a fleeting vision which came to me as a complete surprise. . . . I saw in imagination a solemn pagan rite: sage elders, seated in a circle, watching a young girl dance herself to death. They were sacrificing her to propitiate the god of spring." Stravinsky has always insisted that there is no plot, saying, instead, that it is a group of scenes and ceremonies about pagan Russia. But while there may not be a plot, there is definitely a narrative flow, which builds in intensity to the end. *The Adoration of the Earth* begins with scenes and dances of springtime performed by young girls, moves to the abduction of one of them, and ends with the procession of a sage and a dance of the earth. *The Sacrifice* glorifies the chosen one, evokes the ancestors, and ends with the sacrificial dance.

To create and support these scenes in sound, Stravinsky chose an unusually large orchestra, one using all the regular instruments plus many of the more seldom-used ones as well, particularly in the woodwinds (which require five of each basic instrument), and the percussion (which can require as many as seven lines of score). His unique ways of handling the many voices of this large group, essentially creating from them a single instrument, is one of the innovations that startled the original audience. Because of a scheduling delay by the Ballet Russes, Stravinsky had had almost an extra year to fine-tune his orchestration. And even before beginning, he had already proved he was both an innovator and a master at evoking new sounds from an orchestra. The press, after all, had called *The Firebird* "refined and fragrant music." *Petrushka* it called "stunning, unexpected, kaleidoscopic."

Within *The Rite of Spring*, Stravinky creates several different worlds of orchestral sound. Music for the young girls, for instance, is somewhat more lyrical and melodic, though frequently it is only fragments of melodies that we hear, and these are sometimes played a whole step apart. The music for the abduction and the dances, on the other hand, is obsessed with rhythm and accents, while the elders are portrayed by dark timbres moving in slower, more even paces. And throughout it all, the orchestral effects are dazzling, making each scene come alive, causing the audience to take notice.

Stravinsky on Composing

The faculty of creating is never given to us all by itself. It always goes hand in hand with the gift of observation.

Poetics of Music, 1942

For me, as a creative musician, composition is a daily function that I feel compelled to discharge. I compose because I am made for that and cannot do otherwise.

Stravinsky: An Autobiography, 1936

Musically, Stravinsky makes rhythm and timbre the most important elements of the sound, displacing, but not eliminating, melody and harmony from a position they had held, until Debussy, without challenge. Melody, for Stravinsky, is often only a series of short ideas, or motives, that grow and continue to hold our attention through metrical and rhythmic variations, more so than through changes of pitch. Harmonically, Stravinsky's chords exist almost in isolation, each one standing alone as separate blocks of sound. These new chords can often be analyzed by functional harmony, as Boucourechliev observes, but then asks, "To what purpose?" For in Stravinsky's music, each chord lives in a world of its own, reminiscent of, but outside, the Classical-Romantic harmonic tradition, where never-ending progressions of chords sweep the listener along through various states of mood and emotion. Stravinsky, by contrast, drives his chords, and makes his melodies dance with rhythmic innovations that are among the most striking and original aspects of *The Rite of Spring*. His chords, which repeat rather than progress, pulsate in rhythms that seldom accent the beat we expect. His dances move in meters so irregular and awkward that parts of the score were eventually rewritten to make it easier to conduct. And his sacrificial dance becomes an orgy of rhythm and orchestral color, with accented, polytonal chords stabbing through the air at the listener. To that first-night audience, Stravinsky's rhythms were like nothing they had ever heard before; there was no precedent to draw on when trying to understand them. The rhythms, like the music itself, seemed barbaric, primitive, primeval, pagan.

So what was the riot all about? The shock of the new. New values colliding with those of the past. Stravinsky's pulsating rhythms, bitonal chords, and kaleidoscopic orchestral effects all contributed to a sound—described variously as brutal, savage, and chaotic—that drove that first-night audience to a place few of us ever experience—that moment when something new and original actually unfolds in front of our eyes. In rare times such as these, the view can be blinding, the sound deafening. Some people can't stop laughing. Others want to scream or fight. Today, virtually surrounded by a sea of sound as we are, this is an experience most of us only read about in books. But the audience that night, in the new Théâtre des Champs-Elysées, had the opportunity first hand.

It didn't take long, however, for *The Rite of Spring* to be heard for what it was. Its first success came in less than a year, on April 5, 1914, when it was again performed in Paris. This time, it was a triumph, and Stravinsky was carried out on the shoulders of the crowd. The press said that, "After the last chord there was delirium . . . the applause went on until everyone was dizzy." Later that year, Serge Koussevitzky conducted a concert performance in Moscow. The Vienna premiere, in 1925, did cause a mini-scandal of its own, but by then it was more a comment on the audience than it was on the music. By the time *The Rite of Spring* was played in Tokyo in 1950, people thought it was a masterpiece.

Stravinsky, however, soon abandoned what came to be known as his Russian period, and began writing music in a new, more restrained, neo-classical style, more concerned with balance and order. He continued in this direction until the 1950s, when he changed course once again, adopting the serial technique invented by Arnold Schoenberg. But although he wrote great music in all of these styles, he is probably best known, and some say represented, by his three early ballet scores, based on Russian folklore and written for Diaghilev's Ballet Russes to perform in Paris.

A true citizen of the world, Stravinsky earned much of his living conducting and recording his music, traveling and living in a style few composers have since attained. He began a three-month tour of the United States just after Christmas in 1924, conducting the New York Philharmonic and giving an evening of chamber music at Aeolian Hall on January 25 that included his *Ragtime* for eleven instruments. Stravinsky, too, it seems, had been affected by jazz, but he didn't take to it as naturally as others did. His second tour of the United States began in 1934, and in 1945 he became an American citizen, settling in southern California. By 1962, his fame was such that he was invited to the White House for dinner with the Kennedys. Later that year, he made a long-awaited returned to Russia and was received in Moscow by Premier Khrushchev. Three years later, he was decorated by the Pope in Rome. Igor Stravinsky died in New York in 1971, and his body was taken to Italy to be buried in Venice.

The Rite of Spring, however, lives on, perpetually opening the door, as it were, to the twentieth century. Not only can it still be seen on ballet programs and heard live in concert, it also remains a popular work for orchestras to record. Stravinsky was one of the first composers to recognize the importance of recorded music; he himself recorded *The Rite of Spring* four times. In 1940, Walt Disney used excerpts in *Fantasia*, his animation classic. And in 1987, the Joffrey Ballet of New York gave a revival of the original dance, complete with copies of the first costumes and the recreated choreography of Nijinsky. Once again, pagan Russia, clothed as *fin-de-siècle* American Indians, stomped and danced to rhythms that had driven that first Paris audience into a frenzy. And while it didn't produce a riot, it did make clear to those of us in attendance what all the fuss was originally about. *The Rite of Spring* is one of those self-defining works in a class by itself. It is the sound of the beginning of modern music.

Pierrot Lunaire

ARNOLD SCHOENBERG

1912

For most of this century, the name of Arnold Schoenberg has been embroiled in controversy and scandal. His champions say he gave music a new freedom—even a new direction—by creating a systematic way of writing it, that lifted composers out of the harmonic quagmire of late-nineteenth-century, post-Wagnerian chromaticism. This chromaticism, they claim, had already rendered tonality obsolete long before Schoenberg ever arrived on the scene. His critics, on the other hand, accuse him of trying to destroy music by substituting his own artificial system of composition for the traditional one based on the overtone series—with the unifying idea of a tonic to which all the other pitches are related—a system that had, they point out, been in place for hundreds of years. His most severe critics accused him of violating the natural laws of music, solely, some say, for his own glorification. Schoenberg himself claimed he had achieved the "emancipation of the dissonance," by which he meant that the pitches in his music were no longer related to a tonal center, but only to one another, and all now were equally important. Although passions still run high on this issue, one thing everyone agrees with is that, in Schoenberg, the battle lines

Arnold Schoenberg. *Corbis-Bettmann*

between the new music and tradition are deeply drawn. The battle, for that's what it was (and still is, to some extent), was between tonality and atonality. Through the century, this musical war has been fought at one of the most fundamental levels of music: the attempted redefinition of the concepts of *consonance* and *dissonance*.

Like most iconoclasts, Arnold Schoenberg did not set out to become so controversial. Born in 1874, the son of a Vienna shopkeeper, he began studying violin when he was eight, viola and cello a short time later. He taught himself much of the classical chamber-music literature. His parents were both musical, as was his younger brother, who became a professional singer. Schoenberg's earliest music, which he wrote for his friends, shows the unmistakable influence of Brahms. But his father's death, when Schoenberg was fifteen, seriously altered the situation and forced him to take a job in a bank rather than pursue his education at the university.

In 1894, when he was twenty, Schoenberg became a student (later a friend and later still a brother-in-law) of Alexander Zemlinsky. Zemlinsky, a composer and prominent opera conductor, guided Schoenberg toward Wagner, all of whose operas he reportedly had heard twenty or thirty times each. Before long, Schoenberg's music showed more in common with Strauss and Wagner than it did with Brahms. In later life, however, Schoenberg said that he believed his music reconciled the revolutionary aspects of Wagner with the conservative ways of Brahms.

Schoenberg's first music to attract serious attention was *Transfigured Night*, a sextet for strings written in 1899 when he was twenty-five. A programmatic piece modeled after Strauss, and based on a poem by Richard Dehmel, it tells the story of a couple's love, the woman's sin, the man's forgiveness, and the resultant transfigured appearance of the world. Schoenberg said he was not trying to illustrate the action, only to "portray nature and express human feelings." Although the music uses the chromatic language of Wagner, it remains tonal, with nothing more daring than the then unacceptable inversion of a ninth chord. Nevertheless, *Transfigured Night* was loudly hissed and booed at its premiere (a popular sport for the conservative Viennese audiences of the time).

But while Schoenberg's early music began in the tonal tradition, it was a tonality weakened by extreme chromaticism. The ultimate result of this approach—that is, the clouding of the tonal center with chromatic chords and melodies, and the delaying of harmonic resolutions to the tonic with various kinds of deceptive progressions and cadences—was that the tonal center itself eventually became so weakened and obscured that the relationship between consonance and dissonance actually began to disappear. By 1908, Schoenberg and his two pupils, Anton von Webern and Alban Berg (these three later became known as the Second Viennese School), were writing music that renounced a tonal center altogether. This, in turn, allowed them to treat most dissonances as consonant sounds, since there was no longer any ultimate consonance—the tonic—against which to be dissonant. As Charles Rosen points out in his 1975 book on Schoenberg, this *emancipation of the dissonance* destroyed "the basic harmonic conception of the cadence, the movement toward release of tension, . . . which had been fundamental to centuries of music." By 1911, Schoenberg could say, "We have progressed so far today as to make no more distinction between consonance and dissonance."

At the point where the concept of a tonal center is consciously rejected—an ambiguous musical state known as atonality—the problem becomes one of maintaining musical coherence. Not only does atonality require fundamental changes in how a composer thinks about harmony, it demands the rethinking of melodies and forms as well, since every aspect of a musical work is now decentralized and the "rules" no longer apply. Schoenberg's solution to this dilemma was to turn first to miniature forms, in which everything was highly concentrated, and then to a text or poem as the underpinning for larger forms, since the music could then mirror the character and mood of the words. This, essentially, is what occurred between 1908 and 1913—Schoenberg's great expressionist period—which culminated in his most well-known and often-played work, *Pierrot Lunaire.*

Pierrot Lunaire (Moonstruck Pierrot)—the mythical tortured clown—is a setting of twenty-one poems from Albert Giraud's 1884 cycle of fifty poems of the same name. There is no real story or plot inherent in either the original collection of poems or in Schoenberg's choices. Instead, as characterized by Jonathan Dunsby in his 1992 book on *Pierrot Lunaire*, there is "a succession of images, ideas, actions, [and] moods," much like "the disassociated images of a dream."

Commissioned by the actress Albertine Zehme, this cycle of melodramas (traditionally, spoken texts set to music; a *fin-de-siècle* fad) is written for an actress/reciter, accompanied by a chamber group of five people playing eight different instruments: flute/piccolo, clarinet/bass clarinet, violin/viola, cello, and piano. The variety of instrumental colors Schoenberg elicits from this small group is astonishing. He was a master orchestrator; even his severest critics conceded that.

What is most immediately striking about *Pierrot Lunaire* is not the orchestration, however, but how the voice is used. The voice neither sings nor speaks, but rather intones a speech-melody that glides continuously from one word to the next, a technique Schoenberg called *Sprechstimme*. While rhythm and dynamics are meticulously controlled, the pitch of the voice has a degree of freedom unprecedented in Western classical music, a freedom that makes its own unique contribution to the abandonment of tonality.

If there was a model for *Pierrot Lunaire*, it can be found in a combination of the biting, satirical world of the cabaret, popular in Berlin at the turn of the century, and the morbid, often macabre world of expressionist painting, in which real objects and people are distorted in order to reveal their inner experience and true feelings. (Edvard Munch's *The Scream*, currently available on T-shirts and as inflatable dolls, is probably the best-known example of this genre.) Surprisingly, Schoenberg had an intimate knowledge of cabaret. He lived in Berlin from 1901 to 1903 where he worked as the musical director for a popular nightclub, the *Überbrettl*, conducting, arranging, and even writing songs. The memory of this experience surely played some role in the writing of *Pierrot Lunaire*, as perhaps did the controversial new ideas of fellow Viennese Sigmund Freud. At the least, these factors contributed to what Rosen labeled "a background of controlled hysteria."

Musically, Schoenberg was never trying to write something "pretty." In his mind, music had a higher calling than that. He wanted his music to compel the listener to listen, to concentrate on ideas and emotions; and he often expressed ideas and emotions in exaggerated or distorted ways the better to make his point. In 1911, Schoenberg wrote to the painter Wassily Kandinsky that "art belongs to the *unconscious!* One must express *oneself!* Express oneself *directly!*"

When hearing Schoenberg express himself in *Pierrot Lunaire*, first-time listeners are often surprised by how disjointed it can all sound. There seems to be no point of reference. It's seldom possible to tell a chord tone from a nonchord tone, that is, a consonance from a dissonance. Everything sounds dissonant. Or consonant, since it's all the same thing without a key center. It can even be hard to hear where one chord stops and the next one begins. The casual listener often hears only a jumble of disconnected notes.

In order to control this potentially chaotic situation, Schoenberg turned to the classical techniques of organization that he borrowed from the music of previous centuries. To begin, he sets his work in the traditional form of a song cycle. Then he sets some of the songs in simple dance forms, such as the polka and the waltz; others, he puts in tightly controlled contrapuntal forms, such as the passacaglia and the canon. One song, No. 18, is a "double-fugue with canon and retrograde of the canon," prompting Rosen to remark that it "is one of the most elaborate canons worked out since the end of the fifteenth century." Beyond that, Schoenberg calls upon rhythm—in the form of a short motive that occurs in various guises throughout the twenty-one songs—to supply the unifying element that, in tonal music, would come more directly from harmony.

In spite of all this, however, it can still be difficult, if not impossible, to comprehend what's going on. While this is partly due to the atonal disorientation, it is also caused by the fact that Schoenberg seldom repeats anything, preferring instead to let variation take the place of repetition. In *Pierrot Lunaire*, we never hear the same thing twice. As he admits, "Almost the only aid to one's perception . . . is logic and an acute sense of form." Obviously, Schoenberg had an educated and attentive audience in mind. Needless to say, this attitude didn't sit well with his critics.

Others on *Pierrot Lunaire*

If this is "music of the future," one can only say that Schoenberg is about a thousand years ahead of his time, for the ear, as well as the brain, cannot readily grasp the significance, if there is any, of such music.

Daily Mail, London, 1912

Only a psychiatrist can help poor Schoenberg now.

Richard Strauss, 1913

Every composer has his aura; the aura of Arnold Schoenberg is, for me, the aura of original depravity, of subtle ugliness, of basest egoism, of hatred and contempt, of cruelty, and of the mystic grandiose. . . . If such music-making is ever to become accepted, then I long for Death the Releaser.

New York Times, 1913

From the standpoint of music as developed by Bach, Haydn, Mozart and Beethoven, Schoenberg's *Pierrot Lunaire* is mere trash. Judged as music, it is hideous. It is not the sort of thing that an American audience can enjoy.

Evening Telegram, New York, 1923

The name of Schoenberg is, as far as the British public is concerned, mud.

Musical Times, London, 1930

Pierrot Lunaire was first performed in Berlin on October 16, 1912, and was repeated in two subsequent concerts. Schoenberg said it had required forty rehearsals. The audiences for the concerts were, according to Dunsby, mostly "professional musicians and critics." Stravinsky was there; Schoenberg had sent him a ticket. When the piece was over, and to the astonishment of some, Schoenberg received an ovation. And most of the audience stayed until *Pierrot Lunaire* was performed a second time.

Arnold Schoenberg wrote very little music between 1918 and 1923, saying later that the war "made people think differently about modern music." When he reemerged as a composer, at the age of fifty, it was with a new technique for controlling atonality, which he had invented in 1921. His system, which he called a *Method of Composing with Twelve Tones Which are Related Only with One Another*, involves using all twelve pitches of the chromatic scale before one is repeated, and initially arranging these twelve tones in such an order that, through the classical techniques of inversion, retrograde, and retrograde inversion, one basic set (as he called the arrangement) could generate the musical material for an entire piece of music. Music now completely free from the shackles of tonality. Music in which dissonance is, once and for all, emancipated.

Twelve-tone music, or serialism, as it commonly came to be called, became both Schoenberg's legacy and his curse. Everyone took sides. Even at the end of his life, his music was genuinely hated by many in a way few composers have ever been forced to endure. But in time the battle turned, and Schoenberg had his revenge. In the first third of the century, serialism vied with neoclassicism for bragging rights as the one true way to compose. During the second third, and with the collapse of its competition, serialism became the technique of choice for most composers, and was taught in the majority of colleges and universities throughout America and Europe.

Schoenberg lived the final years of his life in southern California; close to, but not friends with, Stravinsky (whom he had once called "little Modernsky" in a choral piece). The final irony to this turn of events, or perhaps even its trigger, is that shortly after Schoenberg's death, in 1951, Stravinsky suddenly abandoned neoclassicism, and for the rest of his life wrote music using Schoenberg's twelve-tone technique. For a brief but brilliant moment, serialism seemed in control. Fortunately or unfortunately, however—depending on one's point of view—serialism never attracted a large general audience. Even today, it remains the music of specialists. And with the possible exception of *Pierrot Lunaire*, Schoenberg's music is more talked about than listened to, and his desire to be known as "a superior sort of Tchaikovsky," whose melodies are "known and whistled," never quite came about.

5

The Concord Sonata

CHARLES IVES

1911 – 1915

When people first hear the music of Charles Ives, what usually strikes them is how dense it all sounds. Layer upon layer upon layer. Seventeen layers of rhythms, for instance, inside the complex tapestry of his Fourth Symphony. But what strikes them next is how many tunes they often recognize in it: "America," "Columbia the Gem of the Ocean," "Nearer My God to Thee," the first four notes of Beethoven's Fifth Symphony. This music could not have been written in Europe. Then, when they find out Ives really sold insurance during the day, and was quite good at it too, and that he wrote tons of music, almost all of which he never got a chance to hear, they're really mystified. Who is Charles Ives? Why did he do that? How can we begin to understand his enigmatic music?

There is a famous story about General Grant telling President Lincoln that he only knew two tunes: "Yankee Doodle," and everything else. But what no one seems to remember is that the comment was made in a conversation the two were having about George Ives, Charles Ives's father. George E. Ives was the leader of the Brigade Band of the First Connecticut Heavy Artillery, and at age seventeen the youngest band director in the Civil War. The way the story goes, Lincoln, at the siege of Richmond, said, "That's a good band," to which Grant replied, "It's the

Charles Ives. *Corbis-Bettmann*

best band in the Army, they tell me." He then added the well-known quip: "But you couldn't prove it by me. I know only two tunes," etc. This story, which is true according to one of Grant's officers, is important to our story, because it provides an important clue to understanding the rhythmically complex, highly dissonant music of Charles Ives— America's first truly experimental composer, and the transcendentalist father-figure of the 1960s American avant-garde. Because the real key to understanding the music of Ives is first to understand his father.

During the late nineteenth century, when Charles Ives was growing up—he was born in 1874—it was naturally assumed that any American who wanted to become a composer of symphonic music would go to Europe to study. Europe, after all, had been the center of Western musical culture for more than two hundred years. And America, still in its cultural infancy, was highly sensitive to European opinion. No American composer could hope to be a success at home without the proper credentials and stamp of approval from Europe. So American musicians like George Chadwick, Horatio Parker, and Edward MacDowell all trooped off to Europe, preferably Germany, where they learned not only the techniques of classical style, but absorbed the aesthetics of late nineteenth-century European culture as well. When they returned to America—either as conservatives, and followers of Brahms; or as progressives, following Liszt and Wagner—they saw their mission as improving the musical standards of the folks back home. But as Henry Cowell says in his 1955 book on Ives, these old-world European rules of harmony and composition, when transplanted to America, "took on a doctrinaire authority that was the more dogmatic for being second-hand."

Others on Ives

There is a great Man living in this Country—a composer.

He has solved the problem how to preserve one's self and to learn.

He responds to negligence by contempt.

He is not forced to accept praise or blame.

His name is Ives.

found among Arnold Schoenberg's papers after his death, 1951

Charles Ives, by contrast, studied with his father. When the Civil War ended, George Ives returned to Danbury, Connecticut, where he led the town band, directed choirs, taught most musical instruments, and played piano for the dances and the organ for church, becoming, in Cowell's words, a "jack-of-all-musical-trades." But more significantly for his son's education, he also loved to experiment with musical sound, particularly tone clusters, polytonality, and quarter tones, long before these techniques were taken seriously by other musicians. In his notes from the early 1930s, intended for an autobiography, Ives tells of watching his father standing in a rainstorm listening to church bells and then rushing to the piano trying to find the notes between the cracks. He also said the family once had to sing "The Swanee River" in one key while his father played the accompaniment in another, an exercise intended "to stretch our ears and strengthen our musical minds." And although not a composer himself, George Ives taught and encouraged his son to be one, first by knowing thoroughly the rules of harmony and counterpoint, then in having the courage to break them creatively.

Musical experimentation, you see, was a family tradition in the Ives household. Charles Ives grew up with it. It was natural. Ives said his father "had a remarkable talent for music and . . . also a philosophy of music that was unusual." Just how remarkable and unusual his father had been became clear to Ives when he got to Yale. There he studied with Horatio Parker, whom he later characterized as a bright man and a good technician, but one who was "apparently willing to be limited by what . . . the German tradition had taught him." Ives said it was only after he got to Yale that he understood "what a remarkable background and start" his father had given him. The difference in musical personalities between George Ives and Horatio Parker was so great that only three weeks into his freshman year, Ives quit showing Parker any of his experimental music, and resigned himself to doing the exercises. But he didn't stop experimenting; he just began keeping it to himself, a practice he was forced—by the sudden death of his father, and later by an indifferent public—to continue for a quarter of a century.

When it came time for Ives to get a job, however, he, like most young men at the turn of the century, didn't consider music a suitable profession. Although a good musician who had held church organ jobs since he was barely a teenager, and was now well schooled in all the "proper" techniques, Ives knew the music he heard in his head was not likely to earn him a living. As he wondered later, how could he ever "let the children starve on his dissonances?" So in 1898, his Yale degree in hand, Ives went to New York to take a job in an insurance company at a salary of $5 a week. To supplement his income during those first years, he also became organist and choirmaster at the Central Presbyterian Church on

West 57th Street, a significant position for someone only recently out of college. Ives, however, remained in insurance throughout his professional life, forming his own agency with Julian Myrick in 1907, and becoming quite a successful businessman in the process. By the time he retired in 1930, he was widely known in insurance circles for establishing the first training schools for agents, and inventing the concept of estate planning, both still standard practice.

Today, in our age of super-professionalism, it's difficult for us to imagine anyone dedicating himself both to selling insurance and to writing music. But that is just what Charles Ives did. During the day he worked in an office; at nights, on weekends, and during vacations, he wrote music. And he kept at it for twenty years, mostly without ever actually hearing any of the music he was writing. This unperformed music by Ives included four symphonies, four violin sonatas, three piano sonatas, two string quartets, almost two hundred songs, and many smaller pieces for orchestra and piano. Even today, it is difficult to imagine how Ives continued to work in near-complete isolation for such a long time, without the connection to an audience most composers think is essential.

Of all Ives's music, *The Second Pianoforte Sonata "Concord, Mass., 1840–1860"* is arguably his masterpiece. Deeply rooted in his New England heritage, its sources are to be found in the music from his childhood: marching bands, popular songs, hymns, fiddle tunes, ragtime, the melodies of Stephen Foster, and the symphonies of Beethoven. The inspiration comes from his father's sense of experimentation, and the New England transcendentalist writers, four of whom became his subjects. In the sonata, each of the four movements is named for one (or, in the case of the Alcotts, the whole family) of the transcendentalist philosophers living in mid-nineteenth-century Concord: Emerson, Hawthorne, the Alcotts, Thoreau. What Ives does musically is to develop impressionistic portraits of the authors. Ives felt so strongly about these transcendental writers that he wrote a book, *Essays Before a Sonata*, to accompany the music, in which he discusses his beliefs about each writer and about music as well.

The four portraits Ives composes are noticeably different from each other. For Emerson, whom he seems to feel closest to, he creates a large, first-movement sonata form in a kind of prose rhythm with no meter signatures or bar lines, saying in his *Essays*, "It must be remembered that truth was what Emerson was after." For Hawthorne, he wrote a fantastic scherzo, saying "Hawthorne feels the mysteries, and tries to paint them rather than explain them." For the Alcotts, actually a family portrait— and the easiest of the four to comprehend initially—he focuses on the house where they lived and what might have taken place inside it, saying, "We won't try to reconcile the music sketch of the Alcotts with much besides the memory of that home under the elms—the Scotch songs and the family hymns that were sung at the end of each day." And for Thoreau, whom he called "a great musician, not because he played the flute but because he did not have to go to Boston to hear 'the Symphony,'" he creates what Cowell calls "a kind of mystic reflection on man's identification of himself with nature," a slow-moving, ethereal piece given to sudden bursts of excitement.

Musically, Ives used many experimental techniques and devices long before they were "discovered" by other composers. Although he did not know the music of Schoenberg, and had barely heard anything by Stravinsky or Debussy, parts of his sonata occur in several keys at once, or in no key at all, only to have the simple diatonic chords of a hymn suddenly interrupt. And he often has many different rhythms going at once, or sections in asymmetrical rhythms, only to bring forth a moment of ragtime, or a memory of a parade. His textures in the sonata, sometimes so thick we can barely distinguish melody from harmony, will occasionally call for even a few measures from a viola, as in *Emerson*, or the brief sound of a flute, as in *Thoreau*. And the dissonances—consecutive extreme dissonances—appear in ways nobody else had ever used them. He even calls for the pianist to use a 14 ¾-inch board at one point in the Hawthorne portrait, in order to play more notes than the hand can reach. And surrounding it all, there is an almost continuous juxtaposition of styles, creating a musical collage in which simple melodies, complex harmonies, tone clusters, and multiple rhythms all vie for attention. In *The Concord Sonata*, there is always a great deal going on, and very little of it ever repeats.

Although Charles Ives is seldom concerned with classical unity, he does create a sonata that makes musical sense. How he does this is through quotation. The beginning four-note motive of Beethoven's Fifth Symphony—Fate knocking at the door, according to some— appears in all four movements, although never exactly as Beethoven wrote it. From movement to movement this motive changes and transforms, taking on a life of its own. Ives felt free to use this well-known fragment because, like the transcendentalists, he believed great themes are universal, and should continue to grow and expand. In *The Concord Sonata*, the Beethoven motive integrates and unifies the constant stream of ideas that goes by.

While *The Concord Sonata* can seem haphazard and confusing at first, repeated hearings offer new connections and relationships and a deeper unfolding of the work. So much is going on that few people hear everything the first time. But what is slowly revealed to the persistent listener is a unique musical mind, working in isolation from the current European tradition. Ultimately, *The Concord Sonata* is music of deep, personal reflection. Music that is searching, as Ives would say, for something more important than beauty "that lets the ears lie back in an easy chair."

from *Essays Before a Sonata*

Preface
The whole is an attempt to present (one person's) impression of the spirit of transcendentalism that is associated in the minds of many with Concord, Mass., of over a half century ago. This is undertaken in impressionistic pictures of Emerson and Thoreau, a sketch of the Alcotts, and a scherzo supposed to reflect a lighter quality which is often found in the fantastic side of Hawthorne.

Emerson
To think hard and deeply and to say what is thought regardless of consequences may produce a first impression either of great translucence or of great muddiness—but in the latter there may be hidden possibilities.

If a composer once starts to compromise, his work will begin to drag on him. Before the end is reached, his inspiration has all gone up in sounds pleasing to his audience, ugly to him—sacrificed for the first acoustic—an opaque clarity—a picture painted for its hanging.

Hawthorne

There is often a pervading melancholy about Hawthorne, . . . There is at times the mysticism and serenity of the ocean, . . . There is a sensitiveness to supernatural sound waves.

The Alcotts

The Alcott house . . . seems to stand as a kind of homely but beautiful witness of Concord's common virtue. . . . telling, in a simple way, the story of "the richness of not having." . . . And there sits the little old spinet piano Sophia Thoreau gave to the Alcott children, on which Beth played the old Scotch airs, and played at the Fifth Symphony. . . . All around . . . there still floats the influence of that human-faith-melody . . . reflecting an innate hope, a common interest in common things and common men . . . .

Thoreau

In music, in poetry, in all art, the truth as one sees it must be given in terms which bear some proportion to the inspiration. In their greatest moments, the inspiration of both Beethoven and Thoreau express profound truths and deep sentiment.

Epilogue

The humblest composer will not find true humility in aiming low—he must never be timid or afraid of trying to express that which he feels is far above his power to express, any more than he should be afraid of breaking away, when necessary, from easy first sounds . . . .

Although *The Concord Sonata* was finished in 1915, it did not receive a complete performance until 1939 when John Kirkpatrick played it on a concert at Town Hall in New York. Ives, who wrote almost no music after the First World War, had, in 1920, published both the sonata and the essays privately, at his own expense, but that had generated almost no interest in his work. At the time of the premiere, Charles Ives was an obscure composer of whom few people had ever heard. But Kirkpatrick's performance began to change all that. In his review of the premiere, Lawrence Gilman called Ives "one of the great pioneers of modern music, a great adventurer in the spiritual world, a poet, a visionary, a sage, and a seer." Slowly, Ives began to receive the public recognition that had been so long denied him. In 1946, he was elected to the National Institute of Arts and Letters. A year later, his Third Symphony was premiered in New York and awarded the Pulitzer Prize. In 1948, Kirkpatrick's recording of the sonata was issued by Columbia Records and led the best-selling list for several months. Three years later, in 1951, his Second Symphony was premiered by Leonard Bernstein, The premiere of his Fourth Symphony occurred in 1965, conducted by Leopold Stokowski. Ives, unfortunately, had died eleven years earlier, at the age of seventy-nine.

Charles Ives, who had all but quit writing music by 1918, was sixty-five years old when *The Concord Sonata* was premiered; he was seventy-three when he was awarded the Pulitzer Prize. In his typical no-nonsense, New England way, Ives told members of the Pulitzer committee: "Prizes are for boys. I'm grown up." And so he was. And in a way, American music had grown up with him. Because Charles Ives, more than any other homegrown American composer, represents the point where American music takes its place alongside that of Europe as a cultural equal. Today, we speak of four composers whose music defines the beginning of the new century: Debussy, Stravinsky, Schoenberg, and Ives.

6

Rhapsody in Blue

GEORGE GERSHWIN

1924

The concert was billed as "An Experiment in Modern Music," and it took place in New York's Aeolian Hall on February 12, 1924. What made it so special was that the "experiment" was an attempt to legitimize jazz as more than mere dance music by displaying it within a traditional concert-music setting. The man behind this plan was Paul Whiteman, America's self-styled King of Jazz, and the best-known dance-band leader of the early twenties. Whiteman's intention was to "emancipate" jazz (he symbolically set the concert on Lincoln's birthday) by offering it in symphonic arrangements—a specialty of his band—and playing it in a concert hall for an audience of critics, professional musicians, and concertgoers who, until then, at least, had not thought to take jazz seriously. A master of promotion, Whiteman filled the hall (during a snowstorm, no less), and some say he could have sold ten times the available tickets. In addition to all the critics, the audience included Serge Rachmaninoff, Leopold Stokowski, Victor Herbert, Jascha Heifetz, and John Philip Sousa. Everyone, it seems, came to hear what this "experiment" was all about.

The newspaper publicity, which began on January 3, announced new works by Deems Taylor and Victor Herbert, as well as Whiteman's

George Gershwin. *Corbis-Bettmann*

pièce de résistance, a new "jazz concerto" by George Gershwin. According to his brother, Ira, no one was more surprised to learn about this than George. Although they knew each other from their work on Broadway in *George White's Scandals* (Gershwin wrote the music, Whiteman conducted the orchestra), and Whiteman *had* once asked George to write something for his band, nothing was ever agreed upon, and Gershwin, who had other things to do, forgot all about it. But this turn of events intrigued him. He said later, "There had been so much talk about the limitations of jazz . . . [that] I resolved, if possible, to kill that misconception with one sturdy blow." Turning to his notebooks of musical ideas, he found what became the opening theme, complete with its sweeping—unmistakably modern—clarinet glissando. And although only a month remained, he decided to accept the challenge.

George Gershwin was known to work fast, often under quite noisy conditions, but this wasn't much time, even for him. Unfortunately, he also had other obligations during the month, including a concert in Boston accompanying the singer Eva Gauthier. He said that it was actually "on the [Boston] train, with its steely rhythms, its rattlety-bang . . . that I suddenly heard—even saw on paper—the complete construction of the rhapsody, from beginning to end." What he said he heard was a "musical kaleidoscope of America—of our vast melting pot, of our incomparable national pep, our blues, our metropolitan madness." By the time the train reached Boston, "a definite plot of the piece" had come to mind, and within a week of his return to New York, he had "completed the structure, in the rough, of the *Rhapsody in Blue*."

Gershwin on Music

My people are American; my time is today—music must repeat the thought and aspirations of the times.

*quoted by Merle Armitage in **George Gershwin**, 1938*

Before the end of January—only three weeks after he began— Gershwin had finished a two-piano version of the Rhapsody. Whiteman's arranger, Ferde Grofe, said that during those three weeks he had called at Gershwin's home daily to pick up new pages in order to work on the orchestration. By the fourth week, the Whiteman band was rehearsing the Rhapsody at the Palais Royal nightclub, where they played. And a week after that, they performed it at Aeolian Hall, with Gershwin playing the piano.

According to Gershwin, "The *Rhapsody in Blue* presents what I have been striving for since my earliest composition. I wanted to show that jazz is an idiom not to be limited to a mere [three-minute] song and chorus." His intention in writing the Rhapsody, he said, was to take blues "and put them in a larger and more serious form," a form that would give his music a chance to outlive the average life of a song. Twelve years after writing it, Gershwin said that "the *Rhapsody in Blue* is still very much alive, whereas if I had taken the same themes and put them in songs they would have been gone years ago."

The dictionary definition of a rhapsody is that it is a musical group of connected free fantasies, often with an epic, heroic, or national character. There is no one formula or plan for a rhapsody, and sections, of which there can be many, flow freely from one to the other. Gershwin liked to say that everyone who had ever heard the *Rhapsody in Blue* had a story to go with it, except for him. What he meant was that although his rhapsody was certainly capable of eliciting a story, that was not where his interests lay. Gershwin wanted his music to reach beyond the popular stage to the concert hall. In order for that to occur, he knew he needed to work with larger, more complex musical forms, struggling with organic growth and thematic development, rather than relying on the musical formulas of the stage. So in writing *Rhapsody in Blue*, Gershwin focused on the design of the musical structure, not the development of a musical story.

Although Gershwin makes use of dissonances in *Rhapsody in Blue*, they tend to be the more refined dissonances of jazz, in particular the "blue notes," such as lowered sevenths and lowered thirds, or the use of ninth chords and thirteenth chords, a feature of the popular music of the time. But the real strength of the rhapsody comes not from the harmony, or even the jazz rhythms, but from the sound on a concert stage of a dance band from the 'twenties. Even when played by a traditional symphony orchestra, as it usually is these days, the sound milieu of *Rhapsody in Blue* is still that of a society dance band, the orchestration relying, as it does, on clarinets, trombones, trumpets, and saxophones. It was a new sound for the concert hall, and it didn't go unnoticed.

Whiteman's concert that snowy Lincoln's birthday night was long, some twenty pieces in all. And the Gershwin came near the end. But people who were there said the mood of the audience, which had grown restless, changed perceptively when the clarinet began its slow glissando, a sound the *New York Sun* called "a flutter-tongued, drunken whoop of an introduction that had the audience rocking." When the piece ended, the response was overwhelming. The *Boston Globe* declared that Gershwin was "the beginning of the age of sophisticated jazz." And the writer Harry Osgood went so far as to say that the rhapsody was "a more important contribution to music than Stravinsky's *Le Sacre du Printemps*." While few people agreed with that, the result was that the twenty-five-year-old Gershwin, already well known for his songs and his work on Broadway, became world famous, literally overnight. By June, he and Whiteman had made a recording of the Rhapsody. And the following summer, he became the first American composer with his picture on the cover of *Time* magazine. George Gershwin was in the spotlight, and he loved it.

Some people thought it strange that a composer of popular songs and Broadway *Scandals* imagined he could write a sustained symphonic work using jazz. If that was to be done, they reasoned, it would take a *real* composer, like Debussy, or maybe Ravel. Furthermore, the critics were not all agreed in their opinions about the Rhapsody. While some claimed Gershwin had successfully combined jazz with Lisztian romanticism, others pointed out serious shortcomings with the music's form, or complained about his "pretty" harmony, particularly the augmented ninths and chromatically altered thirteenths (to use terminology Debussy and Liszt would have understood). Then there was the reported complaint—from the Russian composer Sergei Prokofiev, no less—that the Rhapsody was nothing more than a string of thirty-two bar phrases, by which he meant a group of songs strung together. And the *New York Times*, while acknowledging "extraordinary talent," had also said Gershwin was "struggling with a form of which he is far from being master." Gershwin, on the other hand, told an interviewer, "I feel things inside, and then I work them out—that's all."

George Gershwin was one of those rare composers capable of bridging the seemingly impossible stylistic chasm separating Tin Pan Alley from Carnegie Hall. Few have ever done it successfully, but Gershwin was unusual. Born in Brooklyn in 1898, he spent most of his childhood on the Lower East Side of New York. A mediocre student, he showed more interest in sports, becoming, according to Ira, "the champion roller skater of Seventh Street." No one in the Gershwin family had ever shown even the slightest musical talent, and it was only after his mother bought a piano for Ira that George's own talent emerged. Ira said George sat down and played a popular song of the day the minute the new piano was hoisted in through the window. No one in the family had had any idea George could play, but they quickly decided he could profit from lessons. And after studying with several neighborhood teachers, he began working with Charles Hambitzer, a composer himself, who taught him to understand harmony, took him to concerts, and introduced him to the music of Chopin, Liszt, and Debussy.

Gershwin was such an extraordinary pianist that at the age of fifteen he quit high school and began working for Jerome H. Remick & Co., for fifteen dollars a week. His job was to play piano for the song pluggers who pushed the publisher's songs. Ira thought George was "probably the youngest piano pounder ever employed in Tin Pan Alley." A year later Gershwin cut his first piano roll, the equivalent of making a CD recording today. He made over one hundred such rolls during the next eleven years. His first published music appeared when he was seventeen. In 1918, he joined the staff of T. B. Harms as a composer, and by the end of the year had songs in three Broadway shows. A year later he wrote his first Broadway score, *La La Lucille*, a show that ran for 104 performances. So by the time he was twenty-one, George Gershwin had earned a solid reputation as a song writer. But the following year, 1920, he had a real hit. "Swanee," a song he had written with Irving Caesar, was recorded by Al Jolson. The record sold two and a half million copies, and earned Gershwin $10,000 in royalties in the first year alone.

Although it would appear that George Gershwin's success on Broadway had caused him to abandon classical music, this was not entirely the case. Off and on, between 1917 and 1921, Gershwin studied harmony and counterpoint with Edward Kilenyi. In 1923, he took several lessons with Rubin Goldmark. Later, he studied for several months with Wallingford Riegger, and between 1927 and 1929, he worked intermittently with Henry Cowell. He even tried to study with both Stravinsky and Ravel, but they turned him down. Ravel advised against it, and Stravinsky reportedly told him it was he who should study with Gershwin, considering the amount of money he was earning. Reportedly, Gershwin had told him it was in the neighborhood of $100,000 a year.

Others on Gershwin

Like a rare flower which blossoms forth once in a long while, Gershwin represents a singularly original and rare phenomenon.

Serge Koussevitzky, 1938

For whatever his flaws, the flaws of George Gershwin are the flaws of America. He mirrored us, exactly. We need only to look into his music to see a whole period of our history exactly stated.

George Antheil, 1938

From the mid twenties to the mid thirties, George Gershwin "bestrode the musical world of Gotham like a young Colossus," to borrow Isaac Goldberg's flowery prose. He continued to write Broadway musicals, most now with lyrics by his brother, Ira. And because of the success of *Rhapsody in Blue*, Walter Damrosch commissioned the Concerto in F, and conducted the premiere with the New York Symphony Orchestra, with Gershwin as soloist. Gershwin also played the Rhapsody in the first of several outdoor concerts in New York's Lewisohn Stadium. In 1928, on a trip to Paris, he watched the Ballet Russes dance *Rhapsody in Blue*, choreographed by Anton Dolin. This was the same trip where he collected auto horns and sketched out his new "tone poem for orchestra," *An American in Paris*, to be premiered later that year by the New York Philharmonic at Carnegie Hall.

By 1934, George Gershwin was a celebrity. His most recent performance at Lewisohn Stadium, conducted by Fritz Reiner, had attracted eighteen thousand people. And in addition to a national tour celebrating the tenth anniversary of the Rhapsody, Gershwin had his own radio series, "Music by Gershwin" on NBC. But the high point of the year was in December, when he was invited to the White House and played for President Roosevelt.

The following year, Gershwin's opera, *Porgy and Bess*, opened in Boston. He called it a folk opera. In the same way that *Rhapsody in Blue* crossed boundaries between popular and symphonic traditions, *Porgy and Bess* blurred the line between opera and musical comedy. This was true even in how it was produced. When it opened in New York, a few months after Boston, it opened not at the operahouse, but in a Broadway theater. Again, there were complaints that Gershwin was incapable of working in larger musical forms. His critics were quick to point out that his arias were ill formed, and his musical shapes were not airtight. But as Alexander Steinert, the vocal coach for the original production, said, "When one examines the first operatic attempts of Wagner, Verdi, or Puccini, one can justly be enthusiastic about Gershwin's first opera." And Gershwin himself said, "I chose the form I have used for *Porgy and Bess* because I believe that music lives only when it is in serious form."

Others on *Rhapsody in Blue*

That night in Aeolian Hall I knew we were set. The audience was electric. You can feel those things in the back of your neck. I felt it then. Critics were there—the best. But they weren't antagonistic. They were friendly. It was in the air.

Paul Whiteman, 1938

In July of 1937, all America was shocked by the sudden death of George Gershwin. It was caused by a brain tumor that had first appeared as vertigo and dizzy spells only five months earlier. As late as June, a medical examination had revealed nothing. But in July, Gershwin slipped into a coma, and despite a five-hour operation, died two days later.

It may come as a surprise to learn that during the final year of his life, George Gershwin and Arnold Schoenberg became close friends. Both were then living in Hollywood: Schoenberg was an exile from

Germany; George and Ira had moved there to write film musicals for RKO. George, who by then painted and collected art, even painted a portrait of Schoenberg. But what the two really shared was a passion for tennis. Schoenberg had a standing invitation to play weekly on Gershwin's court.

Following Gershwin's death, his friend Merle Armitage published *George Gershwin*, a memorial collection of thirty-eight essays and articles. As I read and reread some of these essays, one passage in particular began to stand out. How unusual, I thought, that in 1938 Louis Danz would say: "In the history of the music which has been composed in America, the names of Arnold Schoenberg and George Gershwin may well be linked together. In these two creative geniuses we have the fullest expression of today. Neither one nor the other could play from both sides of the net, but both play famously from the side of their choosing."

Gershwin on The Machine Age

I frequently hear music in the very heart of noise.

quoted by Erma Taylor in **Jones' Magazine**, *1937*

7

Bolero

MAURICE RAVEL

1928

How fast should *Bolero* go? What's the right tempo? That may seem like an esoteric question, but it's not. In fact, it's at the heart of understanding Maurice Ravel, an enigmatic person of "fastidious reserve," even to his friend and first biographer, Roland-Manuel. Ravel, you see, is one of those composers who reveals little, if any, of their personalities in their music. This artistic reserve was mirrored in his personal life as well, making him, in the words of biographer Gerald Larner, appear "self-defensively cool." Even today, it can be difficult to explain his ambiguous attitude toward *Bolero*, a work he called "an experiment." The more we learn about Ravel, it seems, the less we understand.

But back to the question of tempo. Does it really matter so much how fast *Bolero* goes? It certainly did to Ravel. In 1930, when Arturo Toscanini took the New York Philharmonic to Paris, Ravel disagreed about the tempo of *Bolero* so adamantly during the rehearsal that Toscanini reportedly told him, "You don't know anything about your own music." At the performance, Ravel accused Toscanini of taking "a ridiculous pace," and refused to stand and share the applause. Later, he said Toscanini "conducts it twice as fast as it should go."

Maurice Ravel. *Corbis-Bettmann*

And if this question of tempo isn't confusing enough, then consider Ravel's statement to fellow composer Arthur Honegger: "I have written only one masterpiece. That is the *Bolero*. Unfortunately, it contains no music." What are we to make of a comment such as this? Why did Ravel write *Bolero*? And certainly, why is the tempo so critical, if the piece contains no music? The answer, if one is available, probably lies in the Apollonian/Dionysian conflict—the Classical/Romantic polarity inherent in all of us. In essence, the answer is to be found somewhere between what Ravel thought he had written, and what Toscanini, and others, think they hear. Because in *Bolero*, the classical ideas of balance and order collide head on with the romantic tension of wild abandon.

To understand what this means, we need to explore the early forces that shaped Ravel, growing up as he did in the final quarter of the nineteenth century. Although he spent most of his life in Paris—arriving there with his parents in 1875 at the age of three months—Maurice Ravel was born in the Basque region, near the Spanish border. The first music he heard, hummed by his mother, were Basque songs; songs, he said, that continued to haunt him all his life. Roland-Manuel says that to ignore this fact is to miss an essential ingredient of Ravel's character. In an unusually revealing moment, Ravel once told a neighbor that all the talk about him having no heart was "not true, and you know it. But I am Basque. The Basques feel deeply but seldom show it, and then only to a very few."

During 1889, when Ravel was fourteen and newly enrolled in the Paris Conservatory, he visited the famed Exposition Universelle. There, like Debussy (who was thirteen years older), he heard the exotic sounds of the Javanese gamelan orchestra, and attended one of the Russian concerts conducted by Rimsky-Korsakov. Ravel's self-described "profound fascination" with the East was immediately joined by an attraction for this new Russian music, particularly that of Borodin, Mussorgsky, and Rimsky-Korsakov. Closer to home, he had always loved Mozart and Schumann, came to favor Emmanuel Chabrier and Erik Satie for their flaunting of the rules, and, for a time—if the *Le Temps* review of 1911 can be believed—was "entirely under the influence of Debussy."

But according to Roland-Manuel, Ravel's true style as a composer formed as early as 1895, when he was only twenty. And although it was a style influenced by Debussy, it was more classical in approach, consisting of clear, well-defined melodies, supported by a sophisticated tonal setting of chords in functional harmony, existing in complex (but logical) classically inspired forms. Ravel's own particular genius was in the way he was able to control his materials. He was an expert at developing melodic ideas, and erecting complex structures in sound. He was a master arranger, in control of every nuance of orchestral color. His goal was always "technical perfection".

Ravel on *Bolero*

In 1928, at the request of Mme Ida Rubinstein, I wrote a *Bolero* for orchestra. It is a dance whose pace is very steady and uniform, as much in the melody and harmony as the rhythm, which the side-drum beats out all the time. The orchestral crescendo provides the only variation.

Ravel, quoted in Roland-Manuel, 1938

In 1909, Ravel, like other Parisians, was caught up in the splendor and magic of Diaghilev's Russian Ballet, then making its first appearance in Paris. Roland-Manuel said the frenzied dancing, sensual music, and crudely colored decors created a "dazzling confusion" from which a "disturbing beauty emerged." The following season, Diaghilev began commissioning French composers and Ravel was one of the first to be engaged. Eager to write for the Russian company, he accepted a commission to compose a one-act ballet on the story of Daphnis and Chloe.

In retrospect, the story of Daphnis and Chloe, a second-century Greek pastoral romance noted for its eroticism and pagan sexuality, may not have been the best subject matter for Ravel. Diaghilev's ballet master, Michel Fokine, whose idea it was originally, had intended to create a sensual, if not sexual, choreography, with stage imagery taken from pagan scenes found on Greek vases and friezes. Unfortunately, the erotic side of music was unfamiliar territory to Ravel. As Larner puts it, "Overt sexual passion was basically alien to his art." The result of this mismatch was that instead of the sexually charged scenario Fokine had originally imagined, Ravel reworked the material into a "choreographic symphony" in three movements, and in the process successfully separated the music and the dance from their erotic imagery and pagan sexuality. The result is music more symphonic that choreographic, while onstage, sensuality is limited to three brief embraces. In his memoirs, Fokine claimed that he loved Ravel's music from the first, but then admitted that "in some places I . . . felt a lack of virility. . . ." After some delay (Ravel was slow with the score, so it was replaced in the 1910 season by Stravinsky's *Firebird*, and in 1911 by *Petrushka*), *Daphnis et Chloe* was premiered in Paris in 1912, on the same program as Nijinsky's scandalously autoerotic version of Debussy's *Prelude to the Afternoon of a Faun*.

Ravel's emotional distance from his material goes beyond the mere rejection of the sensual. It can also be found in the next work he wrote for the Ballet Russes, the one Diaghilev refused to stage. *La Valse*, completed in 1920, is a choreographic poem in homage to the Viennese waltz, complete with echoes of Schubert and Johann Strauss. Written for a large orchestra, the work surges forward, building through two grand crescendos, designed "to make the listener lose his balance," in the words of Roland-Manuel. Diaghilev, when he first heard it, told Ravel it was a masterpiece, but added, "It isn't a ballet. It's a portrait of a ballet, a painting of a ballet." And Roland-Manuel agreed, saying "Although the painting is skillful enough, it aims at dazzling rather than touching the heart."

Early in 1928, shortly before beginning his first American tour, Ravel was asked by Mme Ida Rubinstein—a former star of the Ballet Russes, now directing her own company in Paris—to orchestrate some music by the Spanish composer Isaac Albeniz for a new Spanish dance she envisioned. The premiere was scheduled for early fall. Since Ravel's involvement was merely that of orchestrator, he agreed. During the summer, however, just as he was about to begin, he learned that exclusive rights to the music had been given to someone else; the Albeniz pieces were unavailable. Ravel was furious. Mme Rubinstein was insistent. The result was that, between July and October, Maurice Ravel, much against his will, composed *Bolero*.

Ravel on Composing

With me composition bears all the symptoms of a serious illness: fever, insomnia, loss of appetite.

Ravel, letter of 1913

My objective, therefore, is technical perfection. I can strive unceasingly to this end, since I am certain of never being able to attain it. The important thing is to get nearer to it all the time. Art, no doubt, has other *effects*, but the artist, in my opinion, should have no other aim.

Ravel, quoted by Roland-Manuel, 1938

I consider sincerity to be the greatest defect in art, because it excludes the possibility of choice. Art is meant to correct nature's imperfections. Art is a beautiful lie.

Ravel, interview, 1924

It's lucky I've managed to write music, because I know perfectly well I would never have been able to do anything else.

Ravel, quoted by Roland-Manuel, 1938

Still unwilling to abandon the idea of orchestration, Ravel wrote a melody with two parts: "altogether impersonal folk tunes of the usual Spanish-Arabian kind" as he characterized it in 1931. He then proceeded to repeat this melody "to the point of obsession," never once varying the harmony, key center, or accompanying rhythm, until the very end. As he told a writer from Buenos Aires in 1930, "This theme, introduced by the flute, accompanied by the constant rhythm of the drum, flows successively through the different instrumental groups in a continuous crescendo." In his article, the writer said, "The theme of the *Bolero*, repeated over and over, is one of those memorable themes that the public sings without wanting to."

This, at least, explains why Ravel thought of *Bolero* as "orchestral tissue without music." To him, it was an orchestration project; it didn't contain any of the musical invention and variety necessary to be true composition. *Bolero*, containing no contrasts, no thematic development, and only static harmony, was, in Ravel's mind, essentially monotonous. And as such, it was ideal for the "long and very gradual crescendo" he planned to craft by means of the orchestration. To Ravel, *Bolero* was an exercise, not about talent and genius, but about skill and technique. He worked on *Bolero* as a craftsman would work on a piece of wood. His interest lay in coloring the melody and increasing the volume on each successive repetition, in such a way that it sounded natural and unbroken throughout the length of the piece.

Ravel once told a writer that *Bolero* was as close as he had ever come to technical perfection. Certainly, the listener's interest is held by the way in which Ravel, the most expert orchestrator of his generation, manages the changing coloration of each new line. Each repetition takes on a brighter color, a richer hue. And as the piece slowly grows larger and larger, through this one great crescendo that sweeps from beginning to end, Ravel knows just when to end it. As Larner puts it: "The friction between melody and mechanism finally causes ignition, the tonality lifts off from C major to E major and, as it falls back, the edifice collapses."

But *Bolero* was more than the piece "without music" Ravel thought he had written. To Mme Rubenstein, *Bolero*, as she now called her ballet, was something entirely different. For the premiere at the Paris Opera on November 22, 1928, she was the only female dancer on stage, surrounding herself with twenty men. Her original intention for the ballet, modified slightly in performance, was a bar scene, where she, as a flamenco dancer, would excite the lust of the drinkers by dancing in wild abandon on the top of a table. Perhaps it's just as well Ravel didn't attend. He was away, giving a recital at the French embassy in Madrid.

With the general public, *Bolero* was an instant success. Orchestras everywhere wanted to play it. It was heard on the radio. The piano version sold out. The royalties rolled in. And Ravel, a mediocre conductor, was in demand, even though Piero Coppola, the first conductor to record *Bolero*, said the piece could be handled by "an automaton." The Russian composer Sergei Prokofiev said Ravel conducted by "wielding the baton with somewhat angular movements and almost surgical precision and *skillfully restraining every attempt to accelerate the tempo.*" And here we are back to the question of tempo again.

So why did Ravel and Toscanini have that argument about the tempo in 1930? Taste and temperament. The disagreement came from the Classical/Romantic conflict between the two men. Not only, it seems, did Ravel insist on a slow tempo, he demanded that this tempo hold absolutely steady, not even speeding up at the end. Coppola explained in his memoirs that Ravel (the Apollonian classicist), wanted the crescendo he had orchestrated—the only interesting part of the piece for him—to grow from "this almost hallucinatory insistence of an immutable tempo." Toscanini (more the Dionysian romantic in temperament), thought *Bolero* should not only go faster, but even speed up toward the end, "in order to obtain an effect of Iberian dynamism," that is, a Spanish intensity. Ravel, the second of six conductors to record *Bolero* in 1930, made a version lasting 15' 50". Toscanini's version, not made until 1939, lasts only 13' 25".

So who's right? Does it really matter which tempo is right for *Bolero*? Yes and no. Yes, if you're a classicist, and think it ought to go the way Ravel said it should. No, if you're a romantic, and lean more toward individual interpretations . Fortunately, we're all in luck. The number of different recordings of *Bolero* currently available is now in the neighborhood of forty, more choices than for any other piece. And the difference between the slowest and the fastest versions has grown greater, now somewhat over five minutes, from 13' 00" to 18' 25". No matter whether you want to observe the orchestration unfold in a planned and ordered way, or give yourself over to passion and wild abandon, there is a recording of *Bolero* that's right for you. Not bad, for a piece of music the composer considered a piece of sleight of hand.

8

Quartet for the End of Time

OLIVIER MESSIAEN

1941

It's difficult to imagine a more inhospitable place to premiere a piece of chamber music than in a German prisoner-of-war camp in the winter of 1941. But that's where it happened, Stalag 8A in Silesia, to be exact. It was there, on January 15, 1941, that Olivier Messiaen's *Quartet for the End of Time*, written for violin, clarinet, cello, and piano, was first performed. Most of the five thousand people in the audience were prisoners. So were the performers: the violinist and clarinetist had been allowed to keep their instruments when they were captured; the Germans had provided a cello with three strings for the cellist. At the last minute, they even found an old upright piano for Messiaen to play.

A prisoner since 1940, when he was captured after only a few months of service, Messiaen wrote the entire eight-movement *Quartet* while in captivity. And although he was thirty-two years old, it was one of his first pieces of chamber music. (Much of his earlier work was for organ.) The meaning of the title—*Quatuor pour la fin du temps*—can be viewed in two different ways. A devout Catholic all of his life, Messiaen took the original idea for the piece from the Apocalypse, and the angel who swears an oath that when the seventh trumpet sounds, "There will be no more Time." The first meaning of Messiaen's title is religious; the

Olivier Messiaen. © *Guy Vivien. Used by permission*

desire, as he says, "to express the marvelous aspects of the Faith." An alternate meaning, however, is less spiritual and more personal. Before being called for military service, Messiaen had begun to invent a new rhythmic language for his music, a method of elongating musical time using techniques he had discovered in Hindu music. In that sense, the title suggests his own attempt to destroy the usual time divisions of traditional music, a practice that engaged him all his life.

Born in Avignon in 1908, Olivier Messiaen had distinguished himself almost before his birth. While pregnant, his mother, the poet Cecile Sauvage, had written a book of poems to him. *The Flowering Soul*, as it was called, became well known, and contributed to his lifelong feeling of a mystical connection between his mother and his own creativity. During the First World War, Messiaen taught himself to play the piano, and even began to compose. That was between the ages of seven and nine. At eleven, he entered the Paris Conservatory. By the time he left in 1930, he had earned year-end first prizes in harmony, counterpoint, fugue, piano accompaniment, organ, improvisation, music history, and composition, the last of which he had studied with Paul Dukas. Within a year, Messiaen was organist at the Church of Sainte Trinité in Paris, the youngest organist in France, at the age of twenty-two.

Messiaen on Music

A piece of music must be interesting, it must be beautiful to hear, and it must touch the listener. These are three different qualities.

interview with Claude Samuel, 1986

This perpetual quest for novelty is, in my opinion, very dangerous because it has prevented the majority of composers from working. You remember the cry of Diaghilev: "Surprise me: I expect you to surprise me!" That statement had terrible consequences!

interview with Claude Samuel, 1986

What endured and what still endures is natural resonance. The tonic triad, the dominant, the ninth chord are not theories, but phenomena that manifest themselves spontaneously around us and that we cannot deny. Resonance will exist as long as we have ears to listen to what surrounds us.

interview with Claude Samuel, 1986

I've listened passionately to the waves of the sea, to mountain streams and waterfalls, and to all the sounds made by water and wind. And I'll even go so far as to say that I make no distinction between noise and sound; for me, all this always represents music.

interview with Claude Samuel, 1986

I insist . . . on responding to an unfounded criticism . . . : that my music is sensual. This is a horrible lie. My music is not sensual; it's simply well harmonized and well orchestrated.

interview with Claude Samuel, 1986

The job of organist involved playing for two or three Masses on Sundays, for Vespers, and for funerals and weddings during the week. He was allowed to play his own music at the noon Mass on Sundays. At other services, he played Gregorian chant, or improvised, or played the classics. From the beginning, Messiaen's inspiration for composing came from three sources: his Catholic faith, his love of nature, and his susceptibility to human love, exemplified for him by the myth of Tristan and Isolde. He often said these were but three aspects of the same idea: divine love. Using these inspirations, which remained central to his work all his life, he created a highly personal music, drawing on material as diverse as Gregorian chant, Hindu rhythms, and the songs of birds.

By the age of thirty, Messiaen was developing his own set of scales, calling them "modes of limited transposition," because they were designed in such a way that after only a few shifts to new pitch levels they would begin to repeat themselves, with no further transpositions being possible. To these he added his own rhythmic system, the essence of which was the replacement of "measure" and "pulse" with an irregular rhythm created by the sporadic addition of fractional note values, usually in the form of dots lengthening the notes they follow. His new system also included a fascination with prime numbers and nonretrogradable rhythms. These last are rhythmic patterns that can't be played backwards because they are constructed like a palindrome and will sound the same either way they are played. The techniques Messiaen explored and developed in his earlier music had all been perfected by 1940, when he wrote the *Quartet for the End of Time.*

From the first sounds of "Crystal Liturgy", the *Quartet for the End of Time* seems different, "essentially ethereal" in Messiaen's words, as if the sounds "approach the listener from the eternity of outer space." To create this feeling, Messiaen frees melody, harmony, and rhythm from their normal relationship to one another, allowing them, instead, to coexist autonomously. In "Crystal Liturgy," for example, both the piano and the cello play "rhythmic pedals." For the piano, this pedal consists of a pattern of seventeen rhythmic values overlaid on a series of twenty-nine different chords. Repeating this pedal causes the same harmony to repeat itself five and a half times during the course of the movement. For the cello, playing harmonics high in its range, the rhythmic pedal is five notes from the whole-tone scale, played in the same order for twenty-two repetitions, as it cycles through a rhythmic pattern of fifteen changing time values. These two pedals move independently of each other, as well as of the clarinet and violin. This technique of cycling a set number of pitches through a different number of rhythms, so that they only come out together every so often (a practice called *isorhythm* when it was used by composers of the Middle Ages), is what enabled Messiaen to create a rhythm, melody, and harmony that could all function in isolation to each other.

Messiaen on his Early Influences

I was the only student at the conservatory who had acquired Schoenberg's *Pierrot lunaire* and Stravinsky's *Rite of Spring;* what's more, I knew and liked several other works of Stravinsky—but I was closer to Debussy. I remained loyal to my childhood loves: Debussy, Mozart, Berlioz, Wagner.

interview with Claude Samuel, 1986

Above this bed of repeated rhythms and pitches, rises the clarinet, playing a melody Messiaen transcribed from birdsong, in this case, the song of the merlin at dawn. Messiaen said he turned to birdsong because, of all the sounds of nature, it is the most musical and easiest to reproduce. Another time, he called birdsong "the true, lost face of music." Sounding almost improvisatory, this clarinet line moves ahead on its own. And while it uses all twelve notes of the chromatic scale, the result does not have the characteristics, or the "serial spirit," of twelve-tone music. Instead, Messiaen's chromaticism is put to the service of the birds. The violin, also reproducing birdsong, moves independently as well, creating a countermelody to the more active clarinet line. But the first movement ends abruptly as the birdsong fades and the rhythmic pedals come to a halt in mid sentence, ushering in a silence Messiaen called "of the heavens."

The second meditation, for that's what these eight pieces really are, is a "Vocalise for the Angel Who Announces the End of Time." It is followed by the "Abyss of the Birds." The fourth is an "Interlude," a trio for clarinet, violin, and cello, and is, incidentally, the first piece Messiaen wrote in prison, before a piano was a possibility. To quote Messiaen's words to the performers, it is followed by the "infinitely slow and ecstatic" "Praise to the Eternity of Jesus." In the sixth meditation, the "Dance of Purity for the Seven Trumpets," Messiaen's use of added note values can most easily be heard. Here, all four instruments play the same fast-moving line together, stretching and contracting each short phrase, often into small groups of five, seven, eleven, and thirteen notes (all prime numbers, it should be noted). For Messiaen, his rhythmic music must disregard "repetition, squareness, and regular division" in favor of a music of free and uneven duration, "inspired by the movement of nature."

To understand fully the seventh meditation, "Cluster of Rainbows for the Angel Who Announces the End of Time," we must consider an additional aspect of Messiaen's musical personality. Messiaen was one of a small group of composers who actually saw colors when he listened to music. He described one of his scales (mode 3, transposition 1) as "orange in a halo of milky white, speckled with a little red like an opal." Ultimately, both his melodies and his harmonies function primarily as colors, allowing them to act independently of each other. Messiaen described the colors of this seventh meditation as "these swords of fire, these blue and orange lava flows, these sudden stars: here is the jumble, here the rainbows!" By contrast, the last meditation, "Praise to the Immortality of Jesus," floats by slowly, the violin oblivious to time, the cycles of chords and rhythms unfolding below. New scales, melodies borrowed from birds, rhythms with Hindu sources, and harmonies repeating in circles were all woven together in a web of mystical Catholicism. Although Stalag 8A was a strange place indeed to premiere a set of meditations such as these, Messiaen said that his music was never heard with such attention and understanding.

Messiaen on Music and Religion

I myself am a static composer because I believe in the invisible and in the beyond; I believe in eternity.

interview with Claude Samuel, 1986

The arts, especially music but also literature and painting, allow us to penetrate domains that are not unreal, but beyond reality. For the surrealists, it was a hallucinatory domain; for Christians, it is the domain of faith. . . . Now, I think music, even more than literature and painting, is capable of expressing this dreamlike, fairy-tale aspect of the beyond, this "surreal" aspect of the truths of faith.

interview with Claude Samuel, 1986

Personally, I don't believe in chance. . . . I don't believe in chance because I am a Christian; I believe in providence and I think that everything that happens is foreseen. . . . Furthermore, I think that in art there is *one* truth, *one* version that is good, a choice made automatically by genius.

interview with Claude Samuel, 1986

Released from captivity a few months after the premiere of his *Quartet*, Messiaen returned to Paris and resumed his work as organist at Sainte Trinité. He also accepted a position as a professor of harmony at the Paris Conservatory. In 1947, he began to teach an analysis class there, but did not teach composition until 1966. Carla Huston Bell, in her book on Messiaen, suggests this was because, in the mid 1940s, most of the senior professors at the Conservatory thought Messiaen was crazy.

But Messiaen's ideas were anything but crazy, and much innovative music was yet to come. In 1949, he wrote what ultimately came to be known as the first totally serial work, the piano piece "Mode de valeurs et d'intensites," from the *Quatre études de rythme*. Building on the earlier twelve-tone system of Arnold Schoenberg, Messiaen serially organized pitch, rhythm, attack, and intensity, thus, theoretically, controlling all aspects of the piece and its performance. But although he used tone rows occasionally, Messiaen was not particularly drawn to twelve-tone music, once saying that he felt the terms "tonal," "modal," and "serial" were "an illusion; . . . phenomena that have probably never existed." While he considered his totally organized music an experiment, others saw it as a validation of serialism, and a point of departure for their own work, particularly the mid-century European avant-garde, and Messiaen's two most famous students, composers Karlheinz Stockhausen and Pierre Boulez.

Throughout the years, Messiaen also continued to collect birdsong, and use it in his compositions. He told interviewer Claude Samuel that the best time to find birdsong was "in the spring, the season of love, and at the right moments, which is to say at sunrise and sunset." Much of Messiaen's music using birdsong was written for his wife, Yvonne Loriod, to play on the piano. In some of his larger works, he has tried to portray the awakening of birds on a spring morning from the hours of midnight to noon, as in *Reveil des oiseaux* from 1953, or to catalog the song of every bird in a particular area, complete with the background sounds of its neighbors, as in *Catalogue d'oiseaux*, completed in 1958.

Messiaen on Rhythm and Time

I aspire toward eternity, but I'm not suffering while living in time, all the less so since time has always been at the center of my preoccupations. As a rhythmist, I've endeavored to divide this time up and to understand it better by dividing it. Without musicians, time would be much less understood.

interview with Claude Samuel, 1986

I feel that rhythm is the primordial and perhaps essential part of music; I think it most likely existed before melody and harmony, . . .

interview with Claude Samuel, 1986

Olivier Messiaen died in 1992, having spent almost his entire life teaching at the Paris Conservatory, playing the organ at Sainte Trinité, collecting birdsong and composing. His last large work was an opera on the life of Saint Francis of Assisi. Premiered at the Paris Opera in 1983, it took eight years to write, and is on a scale with Wagner's *Parsifal*. From the perspective of today, it's not difficult to understand why Messiaen became a father figure to the European avant-garde. Not only did he introduce the concept of totally serial music, he was responsible, as Bell says, "for the most significant development in rhythmic practice in the last three hundred years," a feat he accomplished by "redeveloping the principles of ancient metrics," after a long period of rhythmic regularity. Messiaen, however, preferred to focus his attention on the spirit, and the contemplation of eternity, telling Samuel, "I've always wanted solitude. I taught to earn my living, and I played the organ. Beyond that, I chose to remain alone." Ultimately, that may be what attracts listeners to Messiaen. Not his accomplishments, of which there are many, but the opportunity, all too rare at the end of the century, to observe a brilliant musical mind, placed completely at the service of its Faith.

Messiaen on Musical Color

In a certain sense, music possesses a power that is superior to the image and the word because it is immaterial and appeals more to the intellect and to thought than the other arts. It even verges on fantasy and belongs to the world of dreams. What's more, music and color are closely linked.

interview with Claude Samuel, 1986

Colors are very important to me because I have a gift. . . , whenever I hear music, or even if I read music, I see colors. They correspond to the sounds, rapid colors which turn, mix, combine and move with the sounds.

Tempo, 1979

Since birth, I've been devoted to violet; this seems to be a natural phenomenon, for I was born under the sign of Sagittarius.

interview with Claude Samuel, 1986

9

Appalachian Spring

AARON COPLAND

1944

Open. Honest. Authentic. Sincere. These are words that people use to describe the music of Aaron Copland. *Rodeo. Lincoln Portrait. Fanfare for the Common Man.* These are titles he used in 1942. Some people hear the "wide-open spaces" of the west in Copland, others, the rhythm and tension of the country and the times. But all who know his music agree that it speaks for America—the one we all remember—in a way that sounds unique and true. And if American music came of age with Charles Ives, it took its rightful place in the world with Aaron Copland and his Americana style.

Born at the beginning of the century, Copland was, by his death in 1990, a true statesman of music, known and loved throughout the world. And although he loved to travel—living for a time in Europe, and returning repeatedly to Mexico and South America—he still called himself the "Composer from Brooklyn." Even his first biographer, Arthur Berger, marveled at how easily this Brooklyn-born man of Russian-Jewish descent could feel so at home with material as different as Mexican tunes, Cuban rhythms, cowboy music, and Quaker songs. Berger concluded that everything Copland touched he made his own. He also said Copland never wrote anything he didn't feel in his own emotions first.

Aaron Copland. *Corbis-Bettmann*

Copland on Music

Life seems so transitory! It is very attractive to set down some sort of permanent statement about the way we feel, so that when it's all gone, people will be able to go to our art works to see what it was like to be alive in *our* time and place—twentieth-century America.

Copland Since 1943, 1989

Although Aaron Copland wasn't born on the same street in Brooklyn as George Gershwin, he did study harmony with the same teacher, Rubin Goldmark. And, unlike the Gershwin family, who moved to Manhattan, the Copland family remained firmly entrenched in Brooklyn, the father owning a department store where Copland sometimes helped out as cashier. And although all five Copland children took piano lessons, Aaron was the only one who thought seriously about making music a career. From 1917 to 1921 he studied privately with Goldmark, even though it was obvious from the start that, as a teacher, Goldmark was conservative, and discouraged "commerce with the 'moderns.'" Surprisingly, Copland quickly developed into something of a radical, a fan of such *moderns* as Ravel and Debussy. So by 1919, when Copland showed Goldmark his new composition, *The Cat and the Mouse* for piano, it wasn't unexpected when Goldmark said it was too radical a work for him to judge. Copland said that no one had ever told him about modern music, he had to discover it on his own.

In the spring of 1921, Aaron Copland sailed for France, knowing he needed a change and having read about a new music school for Americans being organized that summer in Fontainebleau. After an initial false start with a teacher from the Paris Conservatory as conservative as Goldmark (who went on to teach at Juilliard), Copland quickly discovered the teacher for him: Nadia Boulanger. He said she had "such enthusiasm and such clarity in teaching," that "you felt you were in very sure hands." Over the next half century, so did literally hundreds of other American composers who—from Copland in the 1920s to Philip Glass in the 1960s—studied with Boulanger.

Copland was so enamored with Boulanger's teaching that he continued to study with her in Paris in the fall, staying, as it turned out, three years, and at one point studying piano with Ravel's friend Ricardo Vines. While there, he also began going to concerts, just at a time, he said, when "Paris was an international proving ground for all the newest tendencies in music." Of particular interest were the concerts Serge Koussevitzky gave at the Paris Opera, where Copland heard the music of Les Six—an informal group of French composers influenced by Erik Satie and Jean Cocteau, and brought together by their dislike of Wagnerian pretension—as well as the music of Stravinsky and Schoenberg, and certainly that of Maurice Ravel.

Copland's own music immediately attracted the attention of the French. When *The Cat and the Mouse* was played in a recital that first summer at Fontainebleau, Debussy's publisher, Jacques Durand, offered on the spot to publish it. (Copland was so flattered he sold it to him outright for $25.) The following year, 1922, the Society Musicale Independente gave Copland his first public concert, and then played his music the following year, as well. And by the time he was ready to return to America, in the spring of 1924, Aaron Copland had a request from

Nadia Boulanger to write her a work for organ and orchestra; she had decided to accept her friend Walter Damrosch's request to play with his New York Symphony. First performed by Boulanger and Damrosch in New York in January 1925, the Symphony for Organ and Orchestra was repeated in February by Boulanger and the Boston Symphony, led by its new conductor, Serge Koussevitzky. With allies the stature of Boulanger and Koussevitzky, the twenty-four-year-old Copland was successfully launched on his American career.

Others on Copland

If a young man at the age of twenty-three can write a symphony like that, in five years he will be ready to commit murder.

> *Walter Damrosch, 1925,*
> *to the audience after conducting the premiere of*
> *Copland's Symphony for Organ and Orchestra*

There is only one Aaron Copland: no one has done more for American music than Aaron.

> *Lukas Foss, 1989*

Berger, a composer himself, suggests that one of the basic ingredients of Copland's personality was his ability "to reconcile opposites" ... to "shift gracefully between extremes." If this is true, then nowhere is it more evident than in the various directions Copland's music took over the next three decades. While jazz influenced some of his earliest work, particularly the *Music for the Theatre* (1925) and the Piano Concerto (1927), Copland's style gradually grew leaner and more dissonant; his chords more jarring and more strident; and his melodies seemed, at times, as immobile as *recitatives*. Nowhere was this new, esoteric style more obvious than in the Piano Variations (1930), a work most listeners thought far too liberal in its use of dissonance; a work many even called austere. Many, but not all. Martha Graham choreographed her solo dance *Dithyrambic* to the Piano Variations in 1931.

Suddenly though, or so it seemed, Copland began writing music of an entirely different sort, music in a simpler, more diatonic style, soon labeled "Americana," and seemingly related, in some strange way, to the illustrations of Norman Rockwell, or the *American Gothic* painting of Grant Wood. This sudden about-face came about because Copland, as he said later, began "to feel an increasing dissatisfaction with the relations of the music-loving public and the living composer." What he had noticed was that the "old 'special' public of the modern music concerts had fallen away, and the conventional concert public continued apathetic or indifferent to anything but the established classics." As he concluded, "It seemed to me that we composers were in danger of working in a vacuum." Furthermore, Copland said he began to realize there was "an entirely new public for music [that] had grown up around the radio and phonograph. It made no sense to ignore them and to continue writing as if they did not exist." His decision was "to see if I couldn't say what I had to say in the simplest possible terms." Not only did Copland consciously simplify his music, making it both more lyrical and more diatonic, he also wrote music for a new and different audience, and even tried to make it more serviceable, creating a "play-opera" for high schools, several ballets on American themes, and a great deal of music for the movies, winning an Oscar for *The Heiress* in 1950. With his way of reconciling opposites, Copland had decided to write music he thought lots of people would want to hear. In its own way, this was a radical idea.

Copland's new, Americana style began with *El Salon Mexico*, a work for orchestra written in 1934 and orchestrated over the next two years. Its success following the premiere in Mexico in 1937 was immediate, attracting the attention of a wide concert and radio audience, and quickly establishing Copland as a "success." The new style continued with *Music for Radio* (Saga of the Prairies) of 1937; the ballet *Billy the Kid* (1938); and *John Henry* (1940). But no work exemplifies Copland's Americana style more fully than *Appalachian Spring*, a ballet for thirteen instruments he wrote for Martha Graham.

The story of *Appalachian Spring* centers on a Bride, her Husband, and the pioneer American spirit of the early 1800s. Graham and her company first performed it at the Library of Congress in Washington in 1944. The set was designed by sculptor Isamu Noguchi, who evoked the farmyard and house with only a fence rail, a wall, a rocking chair, bench, and stump. The stump became the pulpit of the Preacher, danced by Merce Cunningham; the bench held his flock. Erick Hawkins, who danced the Husband to Graham's Bride, said dancing in Noguchi's set made you feel "not on a stage," but in "a whole new world."

Copland on *Appalachian Spring*

Martha's ballet . . . concerned a pioneer celebration in spring around a newly built farmhouse in the Pennsylvania hills in the early part of the last century. The principal characters are a bride and her young farmer husband. After Martha gave me this bare outline, I knew certain crucial things—that it had to do with the pioneer American spirit, with youth and spring, and with optimism and hope.

Copland Since 1943, 1989

When I wrote the music, I had no idea what Martha was going to call it! Even after people learn that I didn't know the ballet title when I wrote the music, they still tell me they see the Appalachians and feel spring. Well, I'm willing, if they are!

Copland Since 1943, 1989

Appalachian Spring should be played cooler than Tchaikovsky and lighter and happier than Stravinsky's *Sacre du Printemps*. My own favorite place in the whole piece is toward the end, where I have marked a *misterioso*. I would tell string players that we don't want to know where the up and down bows are. They must have a special sustained quality there—kind of organlike in sound, with each entry like an Amen.

Copland speaking on a 1974 rehearsal recording

The most striking feature of Copland's new style was his use of folk music, sometimes quoted directly, other times, in variation, or disguise. Occasionally, he even wrote new music that sounded like folk tunes. Berger suggests that folk material was playing the same role in Copland's music then that jazz had played in the 1920s, that is, as source material to be personalized. Copland, more pragmatically, always saw folk music as an additional way of attracting a wider audience. He figured most people already knew the shapes, if not the tunes, of folk songs, so that by using them, his new music would contain a sense of the familiar from the very first hearing. Copland said he chose the Quaker song "Simple Gifts" (written in 1848 and known also by its first line "'Tis the gift to be simple . . .") to use in *Appalachian Spring* because it was ideal for both the scenario and the "austere movements" he associated with Graham's choreography. Historian Gilbert Chase called Copland's handling of the five variations he made of this tune some of the most effective writing in *Appalachian Spring*. He also pointed out that some people were now calling Copland's style "American Baroque." Musicologist Vivian Perlis, who worked closely with Copland, called *Appalachian Spring* "music with a quiet glow."

To create this "glow" Perlis talks about, Copland began using a simpler harmony, in the process rediscovering the triad, and rejecting the current rage to find increasingly dissonant sounds. But while he abandoned complex harmonies, he didn't turn away from the chord formations and orchestral techniques that composers from Chopin to Debussy had designed for their support. These old techniques, applied to Copland's new style, resulted in music with open octaves, and a wide vertical spacing of simple diatonic chords. In addition, Copland began trying to keep his contrapuntal lines as far apart as possible in the voicing. He also created a more transparent orchestral texture through the use of a lighter instrumentation, and he tried to use as little chromaticism as possible. For many people, this new sound, full of familiar tunes and wide-open intervals in diatonic harmony, sounded authentically American.

If *El Salon Mexico* brought Aaron Copland's name to public attention, *Appalachian Spring* made him famous. Saying it had "a mysterious coolness and freshness," Edwin Denby of the New York *Herald Tribune* called the ballet an "astonishing evocation of that real time and place. . . . a feat of genius," and referred to Copland's score as "a marvel of lyricism, of freshness and strength." Within the year, Copland made an orchestral suite from the music for the ballet, and it was performed by orchestras everywhere. After the premiere by Rodzinski with the New York Philharmonic, Koussevitzky performed it in Boston, and Leonard Bernstein in London in 1946. The day World War II ended in Europe— May 8, 1945—the front page of the *New York Times* announced that *Appalachian Spring* had won Copland a Pulitzer Prize.

Martha Graham on *Appalachian Spring*

The ballet has to do with roots in so far as people can express them, without telling an actual story.

1943 letter to Copland

During the late 1940s, Copland's musical path seemed both certain and secure. But by the early 1950s, several unexpected developments changed all that. The first, perhaps the result of fame, was that Copland, Americana and all, came under fire from Senator Joseph McCarthy, who accused him of harboring Communist sympathies. A Congressman Busbey from Illinois, it seems, had questioned including Copland's *Lincoln Portrait*—a work for speaker and orchestra that includes the words of Lincoln, a principal theme based on "Springfield Mountain," and snatches of popular tunes from the Civil War—in the concert for Dwight D. Eisenhower's inauguration in 1953. As Busbey told Congress, "There are many patriotic composers available without the long record of questionable affiliations of Copland. The Republican Party would have been ridiculed from one end of the United States to the other if Copland's music had been played." Copland's response, made through the newspapers and the radio, was that this was the first time, as far as he knew, "that a composition has been publicly removed from a concert program in the United States because of the alleged affiliations of the composer." He also said that while his politics—tainted or untainted— would surely die with him, his music "might just possibly outlive the Republican Party."

Copland on Composing

The plain fact is that the composer of our century has earned the right to be considered a master of new sonorous images. Because of him music behaves differently, its textures are different—more crowded or more spacious, it sings differently, it rears itself more suddenly and plunges more precipitously. It even stops differently. But it shares with older music the expression of basic human emotions.

The New York Times Magazine, 1955

The other unexpected event of the 1950s was that Copland suddenly abandoned his simplified style, and began composing using Arnold Schoenberg's 12-tone technique. Copland had not, it seems, entirely abandoned the idea of chromatic music, and has said that by the time of *Appalachian Spring* and his Third Symphony of 1946, he felt that he "had gone as far as I could" with the Americana style. A composer who didn't like being pigeonholed—"I wouldn't want to be thought of as a mere purveyor of Americana"—Copland's own brand of 12-tone writing, essentially more melodic than most, first appeared in his Quartet for Piano and Strings (1950). This unfortunate return to austerity, as many people heard it, reached a climax with the *Piano Fantasy* (1957), a long, complex, and difficult work seldom played today. His *Connotations* for orchestra, written in 1962 for the opening of Philharmonic Hall at Lincoln Center, has fared little better.

Of all Aaron Copland's music, nothing has proved more lasting than the music he wrote in his Americana style. And of that, the piece played the most is *Appalachian Spring*. Used as source material for the main theme of CBS Reports during much of the 1960s, *Appalachian Spring* became the mid-century anthem for what was good and right about America. And Copland, the one composer everybody knew, would surely have become America's composer laureate, if such an honor actually existed. Eight years before he died, Copland told interviewers Gagne and Caras that it was difficult for him to think of *Appalachian Spring* "without seeing in my mind's eye the dancing that goes with it," con-cluding, "There aren't many Martha Grahams in the world, with that much personality and imagination, and the American quality which she gives most of her things." The same, of course, could be said of Copland. Ultimately, Berger was right: the most important facet of Copland's musical personality was his ability to "shift gracefully between extremes." At the time, Copland's fans didn't seem to mind that his style had zigzagged through the century in a way unequaled by anyone except, perhaps, Stravinsky. Today, these twists and turns of style seem merely to reflect the uncertainties of the times, an uncertainty that was, and is, stilled by the "quiet glow" of music like *Appalachian Spring*.

10

Sonatas and Interludes

JOHN CAGE

1948

Who is John Cage? Everyone knows his name. And most people have an opinion about him, whether they've actually heard any of his music or not. In fact, Cage may be the most controversial and misunderstood composer in the history of music. Even today, long after his death at the age of seventy-nine in 1992, many people, including a lot of good musicians, still think of him as "the king of anything goes," a charlatan who almost destroyed the art of music by accepting just any old noise that came along into his musical fabric. Other people still feel a need to diminish his musical accomplishments by claiming that he was a far better thinker and philosopher than he was a composer. While yet others, myself included, think he was the greatest composer of the second half of the twentieth century, a person so influential that he changed forever the way we write, hear, and understand music. So addressing the question *Who is John Cage?* is a far more complicated affair than it would at first appear. The answer you get, it seems, depends in no small part on whom you ask.

But if explaining Cage is tricky, identifying what he did that often confused and infuriated people is not. The facts are clear. John Cage was a musical experimenter who stayed on the leading edge of the

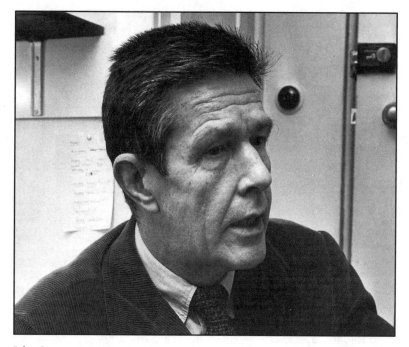

John Cage. *Corbiss-Bettmann*

avant-garde for over fifty years. Many of the musical sounds we take for granted today began with him. Over the course of his career, he introduced into music a number of sounds previously considered noise. These include percussion sounds, electronic sounds, chance-produced sounds, and the sounds and noises of everyday life. In the early 1950s, he became notorious for writing *4′33″*, a silent piece (usually performed on piano), in which no sounds are intentionally produced for four minutes and thirty-three seconds. He said he was encouraged to do this by the solid white paintings of his friend Robert Rauschenberg. Later in the decade, Cage even began to question the very purpose of music, writing pieces completely by chance, letting sounds be themselves, and asking questions about music that no one had ever asked before (often with the help of the ancient Chinese book of divination, the *I Ching*). He did all this, as he would say, to help us still our egos, and "wake up to the very life we are living."

Cage on Hearing Music

I don't have an ear for music, and I don't hear music in my mind before I write it. And I never have. I can't remember a melody. A few have been drummed it into me, like "My Country 'Tis of Thee," but there will come a point in even those songs when I'm not sure of how the next note goes.

Talking Music, 1995

Throughout his own life, Cage considered himself a musical inventor, saying that he always knew this was the area of music where he could make a contribution. His father had been an inventor, and Cage grew up with new inventions constantly occurring at home, in much the same way that Charles Ives grew up with, and was influenced by, the musical experiments of his father. For Cage, finding the next step became a lifelong goal. And although he began music in a fairly traditional way, studying with both Henry Cowell and Arnold Schoenberg, he quickly began to explore beyond the traditional boundaries. His work with Schoenberg, for example, whom he convinced to teach him free of charge by promising to devote himself to music, led to his own unique method of 12-tone writing and the invention of a 25-tone row that spread over two octaves. And his involvement with percussion music, encouraged by Cowell at a time when it was still a novelty, resulted in a large group of new works by Cage and others, and a series of landmark concerts in San Francisco. A similar percussion concert at the Museum of Modern Art in New York in 1943, with musicians performing on such "instruments" as gourds, ox bells, automobile brake drums, and the jawbone of an ass, gained Cage even more notoriety, particularly when pictures of the performance appeared in *Life* magazine.

Cage's fascination with percussion instruments and noise may have developed from two very different sources. The first was his contact with Oskar Fischinger, a pioneer abstract filmmaker, who had the whimsical notion that all inanimate objects possess a soul that is expressed only when that object makes a sound. The second was his growing conviction that percussion music, that is, music without a fixed-pitch reference, would serve as a transition from the keyboard-influenced music of the past to the "all-sound music of the future." For Cage, noise, which is always present in our lives, is disturbing when ignored, but fascinating when listened to. As he put it, "We want to capture and control these sounds, to use them not as sound effects but as musical instruments." He also said, "At the present stage of revolution, a healthy lawlessness is warranted."

Cage on Performance

I don't mean by the silent piece, or any other, that I accept all the intentional self-expressive actions and works of people as suitable interruptions . . . . I don't believe the line that a bad, thoughtless, undevoted performance of one of my works is a performance of it.

Talking Music, 1995

Cage worked with percussion music for almost a decade, first in California, then in Seattle at the Cornish School where he organized a percussion orchestra, encouraged composers to write new pieces, and gave concerts throughout the area. While in Seattle, he was asked by dancer Syvilla Fort to write the music for a new dance she called *Bacchanale.* This presented Cage with a dilemma since the hall where it was to be performed was too small to accommodate his percussion orchestra, and his piano music, which was still 12-tone in style, was inappropriate to the nature of Fort's dance. His solution, discovered only days before the performance, was the invention of the prepared piano.

Basically, the prepared piano is an ordinary grand piano whose sound has been altered by placing such objects as screws, bolts, and pieces of wood, rubber, and weather-stripping between the strings. This has the effect of drastically altering the acoustical characteristics of the instrument, to the point where it is all but unrecognizable as a piano. Instead, these preparations create a range of sounds, each of a different timbre, moving from the lower to the higher octaves without the pitch characteristics of scales and modes. Cage immediately saw this new instrument as "a percussion orchestra under the control of a single player."

After writing *Bacchanale* for Fort in 1940, Cage did not experiment again with the prepared piano until 1943. At that point, he was living in New York and finding it far more difficult to recruit players for his percussion group than it had been on the West coast. So between 1943 and 1949 he turned his attention once again to the prepared piano, writing fifteen pieces during that period that either featured or incorporated the instrument. Of these, the most significant is the *Sonatas and Interludes* for solo prepared piano.

In writing *Sonatas and Interludes*, Cage created a large, hour-long, formal design out of twenty short musical ideas. To control these short ideas he chose an AABB binary format for all but three of the sixteen sonatas. AABB is a relatively simple musical structure, similar in design to the binary forms that Italian composer Domenico Scarlatti wrote harpsichord sonatas in three hundred years earlier. According to Cage, "The first eight, the twelfth, and the last four sonatas are written in AABB rhythmic structures of varying proportions, where the first two interludes have no structural repetitions." He goes on, "This difference is exchanged in the last two interludes and the sonatas nine through eleven which have respectively a prelude, interlude and postlude." Of the four interludes, the first two are in a free form without repetition, while the last two are written in a 4-part form of AABBCCDD.

Of course, the traditional relationship between the look of the score and the actual sounds made during a performance does not exist in *Sonatas and Interludes*. Unlike Scarlatti's sonatas, which can be imagined in the mind from looking at the notes on the page, Cage's notation for *Sonatas and Interludes* is a recipe for actions to be made by the performer, not sounds to be heard, since few keys, when struck, produce the actual notated sound that is indicated on the page. It was this removing of pitch—and by implication, harmony—from music, that caught the attention of most listeners. And Cage, it should be remembered, had for some time been more interested in organizing rhythm and tone color than he was in organizing pitch.

And as surprising as it may seem today, some listeners heard a relationship between Cage's music for the prepared piano and Arnold Schoenberg's 12-tone music. Perhaps, as composer Peggy Glanville-Hicks suggested, this was because "Cage, in changing both the timbre and pitch of every note, gives an absolute identity to each." Or perhaps they heard a similar lack of a clearly defined tonal center, and the absence of recognizable chords moving in recognizable patterns. Other listeners of the time were reminded of Debussy, not because of harmony (of which there was none), but in the delicate nature of the sounds, reflecting as they did an interest in Eastern art and, perhaps, the gamelan. Yet others could hear the rhythms of Igor Stravinsky. But no one accused Cage of imitation; instead, many felt he had gone too far.

Sonatas and Interludes, written between 1946 and 1948, consists of twenty short pieces—sixteen sonatas and four interludes—requiring a little more than one hour to perform. The preparation of the piano is elaborate, altering a total of forty-seven different tones, and requiring two to three hours to complete. The majority of these twenty pieces are written in a rhythmic structure based on duration that Cage invented to replace the traditional role of harmony as an organizing principle, since harmony, as Cage quickly discovered, was inhospitable to nonpitched sounds. Basically, the structure he devised was focused, not on pitches, but on the duration and subdivision of actual amounts of time. For Cage, the advantage of working with a structural organization based on lengths of time was that "nothing about the structure was determined by the materials which were to occur in it." In other words, the structure could be expressed just as easily by the absence of sound, as by its presence. Cage saw this way of organizing time as a structural element and a proper concern of the mind, meaning that it must be planned in advance. The actual sounds and silences chosen to fill these spaces of time he saw as more spontaneous, and belonging to the heart. According to him, the actual preparations for the piano "were chosen as one chooses shells while walking along a beach." The music itself he discovered by improvising at the piano.

Sonatas and Interludes was premiered by pianist Maro Ajemian in New York's Carnegie Hall in January 1949. For many people, particularly audiences of the 1950s, listening to a performance of Cage's prepared piano music was one of the most unusual and unsettling concert experiences they had ever had. The appearance of the piano on stage was unchanged, as was the performer's approach to playing the instrument. But instead of hearing traditional piano sounds, the listener heard metallic rattles, shimmers, plunks, and thuds—"noises" rich in sound, but without a historical or cultural context. Laughter, anger, and bewilderment were common responses. Others, however, heard sounds of profound beauty that spoke to the mood and tenor of the times, showing the way to the music of the future, just as Cage had predicted. Perhaps this is what encouraged both the National Institute of Arts and Letters and the Guggenheim Foundation to give Cage awards later in 1949. The Institute award cited him for having "extended the boundaries of musical art."

Cage on Education

I don't believe in education. I don't believe in things being explained or understood. I believe in things that are inexplicable.

Talking Music, 1995

During the late 1940s, when he was writing *Sonatas and Interludes*, Cage was also becoming aware of Eastern thought, studying first Indian music with Gita Sarabhai, and later Zen with Daisetz T. Suzuki. At first, Cage noticed that his concept of rhythmic structure was similar to the Indian rhythmic system known as *tala*. His interest in Eastern thought became even greater, however, when he learned that the Indian concept of the function of music—to sober and quiet the mind, thus rendering it susceptible to divine influences—had been echoed by Thomas Mace, a seventeenth-century English composer. According to Cage: "I decided then and there that this *was* the proper purpose of music." He went on to conclude that "the Renaissance idea of self-expressive art was therefore heretical." Later, he said that "the self is not really expressed when it expresses itself."

At about the same time, Cage also came to accept the doctrine about art set forth by Ananda K. Coomaraswamy, that the function of art is to imitate Nature in her manner of operation. It was but a short step from there to Cage's conclusion that "our business in living is to become fluent with the life we are living, and art can help this." For this to be possible, Cage felt it necessary to reject the continued production of masterpieces in favor of "a purposeful purposelessness or a purposeless play." For Cage, however, this play represented an affirmation of life, "a way of waking up to the very life we are living."

In order to insure purposelessness in music, Cage felt the composer must realize the difference between entering into music and having something emerge from music. According to him, "The difference is this: everybody hears the same thing if it emerges. Everybody hears what he alone hears if he enters in." The key to producing this nonintentional music was that sounds must be allowed to be just sounds. While Cage recognized that this might, at first, appear to be the giving up of music, he suggested that "this psychological turning leads to the world of nature, where, gradually or suddenly, one sees that humanity and nature, not separate, are in this world together; that nothing was lost when everything was given away." He concluded that, in musical terms, "any sound may occur in any combination and in any continuity." He also suggested that "sounds, when allowed to be themselves, do not require that those who hear them do so unfeelingly."

In order to produce nonintentional music, Cage decided that he must remove his personality from the act of composing. In order to do this, he turned first to magic squares, then to the *I Ching*. The *I Ching*, also called the *Book of Changes*, was written in about the twelfth century B.C.E. It was first an ancient Chinese book of oracles, but deepened in meaning into a book of wisdom and philosophy, eventually becoming the philosophical source for both Confucianism and Taoism. Cage said that the moment he opened the book he immediately saw a connection to his own work. The first piece he wrote by consulting the *I Ching* was the *Music of Changes* of 1951.

The following year, Cage wrote his silent piece, *4′33″*. The label "silent," however, is a misconception. It is not a silent piece, but a piece in which accidental sounds inherent in the performance situation are allowed to be themselves, free from the demands of harmony and form.

It is this admission of environmental sound into musical sound that gives *4´33˝* its importance. Cage, on the other hand, would say the importance is not so much the admission of environmental sounds into music, as the admission of music into life. According to him, "art silence is not real silence," but the whole world of sound, presenting to those who will listen, "nature in her manner of operation."

If all this is beginning to sound a little convoluted, imagine what listeners must have felt in the 1950s. How was it possible, for instance, to reconcile in one's mind the music of John Cage with that of, say, Aaron Copland? In such a comparison, Cage's music suffered, and he was derided, ridiculed, and held up to contempt throughout most of the decade. In the 1960s, however, with the worldwide advent of the avant-garde, things changed. More and more, Cage was in demand at concerts and festivals around the world, first in Europe and then Asia, particularly Japan, where he came to be revered. His experimental attitude became the model for composers everywhere. By the end of the 1960s, Cage was universally regarded as the father of the avant-garde, even by his detractors.

So who is John Cage? It still depends on whom you ask. But more and more, he is being recognized as a great creative artist who extended the boundaries of music farther than anyone had ever thought possible, bringing noise into music, and music into life. A composer who thought music could actually improve our lives, Cage focused our attention on both the purpose of writing music and the primary role of the composer. He offered us the opportunity to listen to our surroundings in a unique way. And did all the controversy bother him? Yes and no. As he said, "If one feels protective about the word 'music,' protect it and find another word for all the rest that enters through the ears."

11

Mysterious Mountain

ALAN HOVHANESS

1955

In the history of twentieth-century music, Alan Hovhaness is an enigma. Within a musical climate of increasing chromaticism and complexity, he has charted his own course through the century, preferring mystery and beauty over what he called snobbish intellectualism. As he told a writer for *Down Beat* magazine in 1982, "Difficult and complicated music doesn't interest me if I can't make it beautiful." He told the same writer that the reason he went his own way as a composer was because he "wanted to write music which was more universal and melodic." A decade later, he told someone else: "I don't want to write like other people."

No one, of course, has ever accused Alan Hovhaness of trying to write like other people. In the first place, he has composed far more music than anyone currently alive. And although composers from the past such as J. S. Bach or Georg Philipp Telemann of the Baroque period, or the French composer Darius Milhaud from our own century have written massive amounts of music, Hovhaness may be the most prolific composer in history, with close to six hundred works to his credit, not counting the more than two hundred pieces—including seven symphonies, five string quartets, and several operas—that he reported destroyed in the early 1940s when he decided to alter his compositional

Alan Hovhaness. *From Crystal Records CD805. © Crystal Records 1980. Used by permission*

style. "The music just suddenly comes," according to him, and he always carries a notebook with him to capture the ideas, writing in restaurants, at the counters of coffee shops, and even in supermarkets, where he jots down melodies while his wife shops. He says that for him, "composing is just a part of life." A waitress who has seen him work this way says the music "just flows out of him."

Hovhaness on Music

Music is a religious thing to me. It has much to do with striking the deeper parts of the human being, the deeper feelings of the soul and mind, as well as uniting man with nature itself.

Tower Pulse, 1991

I think music, especially certain seven-tone scales, is based very much on cosmic laws that affect all life and creation.

Tower Pulse, 1991

The other reason Hovhaness's music is so unlike that of other composers is that, early on, he was significantly influenced by the Orient, finding a unique way to synthesize ideas from the East with the more traditional approaches of the West. Of Armenian ancestry, Hovhaness turned toward that part of the world for inspiration, becoming, by the mid-1940s, one of the first Western composers to blend East and West successfully. Later, he traveled to India, Japan, and Korea, absorbing and incorporating ideas from these cultures into his own music, particularly the many exotic scales and cross-rhythms of Indian music. In 1984 he told musicologist Don Gillespie that he thought that the Indian musical influences were "just as strong as the Armenian influence, perhaps even stronger." The result is unique music of profound and simple beauty described by people the world over as thrilling and inspiring. What is even more astonishing is that Hovhaness opted for this simplified approach toward beauty and spirituality at a time when the majority of his contemporaries were embracing atonality as the method of the future.

Alan Hovhaness was born in Somerville, Massachusetts, in 1911. His father was of Armenian descent and taught chemistry at Tufts University in Boston; his mother was Scottish. Hovhaness said both parents were terrified he would become a composer because they considered music such a pauper's profession. But he began hearing music in his head at an early age, and by the age of four had already tried to compose. His mother discouraged him, however, so he stopped for a few years. But he was improvising at the piano long before he began formal lessons at the age of nine. And by the age of thirteen, he had written two operas. Hovhaness said he studied the works of Handel throughout his teens, slowly purchasing the entire collection of Handel's music with his allowance.

Hovhaness on Composing

I have so many beautiful ideas. I must write them down. I can't stop composing. I have more ideas than I can ever use.

1979

I've always heard the orchestra and everything, all the details, in my head. But then, as soon as I compose the symphony I forget all about it.

Alan Hovhaness (film), 1984

I don't think about a program when I write. In fact, most of these titles come up after the piece is written.

Peter Westbrook, **Down Beat,** *1982*

I like mysterious sounds.

Alan Hovhaness (film), 1984

After attending Tufts University for two years, Hovhaness was given a scholarship to the New England Conservatory, where he studied composition with Frederick Converse, beginning in 1932. His first real success as a composer came when Leslie Heward conducted his Symphony No. 1 (*Exile*) with the BBC Symphony in London in 1939. It wasn't really his first symphony, however; Hovhaness had already thrown that one away, shortly after it won the Endicott Prize at the conservatory in 1933. His work from this early period shows an influence of Renaissance music—although it is written primarily in the harmonic language of late Romanticism—but the initial influences of both Bartók and the Orient can, from time to time, also be detected. It was also during the 1930s that Hovhaness first came under the influence of Indian music, hearing Vishnu Shirali perform with the dancer Uday Shankar in Boston in 1936. Hovhaness said the experience "had a tremendous influence on me."

During the summer of 1942, and feeling a need to gain more control over his technique, Hovhaness decided to attend the summer course at the Berkshire Music Center in Tanglewood, Massachusetts. He was supposed to study composition with the Czech composer

Bohuslav Martinu, but a serious fall early in the summer made it impossible for Martinu to teach. Instead, Aaron Copland led the composers' seminar, assisted by Leonard Bernstein. It was at Tanglewood that summer that Hovhaness first encountered the ridicule and hostility that his music was to provoke in certain composers throughout much of his life. And of all people, the condemnation came from Copland and Bernstein. According to Hovhaness, it began when the seminar listened to an acetate recording of his first symphony. To his surprise, "Copland talked loudly all the way through it." And Bernstein, when the recording was finished, went to the piano, played the harmonic minor scale on which the symphony was based, and said, "I can't stand this cheap ghetto music." Hovhaness, who was both angered and distraught over these actions and remarks, decided to quit Tanglewood, even though he was there on a scholarship, and return immediately to Boston. Disgusted by the experience, he destroyed hundreds of his early works.

There was, however, one good aspect of Hovhaness's Tanglewood experience. His unexpected return to Boston in the middle of the summer made it possible for him to meet the Greek psychic and mystic painter Herman DiGiovanno. DiGiovanno, whom Hovhaness has referred to as his teacher, convinced him to study in depth the music of his Armenian ancestors. This study led Hovhaness, not to folk music, which he felt had been weakened by too many outside influences, but to the purer music of the church. He also became enamored with the music of Komitas Vartabed, an Armenian composer-priest who died in Paris in 1936, and whom Hovhaness called the Armenian Bartók.

Others on Hovhaness

The compositions of Alan Hovhaness are like Japanese scrolls. As they are rolled out, they reveal new images and their message bit by bit. Western music in comparison is like a photographic print.

Time magazine

As these Eastern influences became stronger, Hovhaness's music changed drastically. It grew more rhythmically active and more contrapuntal, and his melodies took on the improvisatory character of Armenian church melodies, as he incorporated the scales and modes of the East. Also, his harmonies became far more consonant than they had been, although in a modal rather than a tonal way, and large sections of his work became, at times, harmonically static. And his rhythm, which has always been considered the most complex aspect of his work, began to utilize long repeated patterns, similar to both Indian talas and the isorhythmic formulas found in Renaissance music.

During the 1940s, Hovhaness lived in Boston, supporting himself by teaching, accompanying performers on the piano, and playing organ at the Armenian church in Watertown. In an effort to better understand Oriental thought, he learned the Armenian language and read Oriental philosophical and religious writers. Gradually, his continued study of Armenian music led him to explore the music of other Eastern cultures. Hovhaness gave his first performance in New York in 1945, playing several of his piano works on an all-Hovhaness program sponsored by the Armenian Students Association of America.

A grant from the National Institute of Arts and Letters in 1951 allowed Hovhaness to move to New York. In the years that followed, he wrote a ballet score for Martha Graham, which she premiered in London in 1954 and then toured to the Far East; wrote the music for a Broadway show by Clifford Odets; and, in 1956–57, wrote the music for two film documentaries for NBC-TV. Although still operating largely outside of traditional musical circles, which continued to shun him, Hovhaness's reputation and success continued to grow, and he was awarded Guggenheim Fellowships in both 1953 and 1954, and again in 1958.

Hovhaness on his Influences

I have always loved his [Sibelius's] music. When I first heard the Fourth Symphony as a child, I remember feeling that this man has said it all— he hasn't left anything for me to say."

Vance Wolverton, *Choral Journal*, 1993

There is a lot of music which has been important to me, particularly Handel, and Oriental music. But I have almost been more influenced by someone who was not so much a musician as a great mystic—Francis Bacon. He was a very great man, and all his philosophical works are dedicated to what he calls the Angelic Intelligences. I like that idea very much. I believe that this is the kind of music which I would like to produce if I could. I try to do that. I fail every time, but I try.

Peter Westbrook, Down Beat, 1982

Although Hovhaness continued to be ignored by the northeastern neoclassical establishment, musicians in other parts of the country began to take an interest. He had already been commissioned by the Louisville Orchestra when conductor Leopold Stokowski, a champion of Hovhaness's music since 1942, ask him to write a work for his opening concert with the Houston Symphony. The result, completed in 1955, was Symphony No. 2, Op. 132 (*Mysterious Mountain*), Hovhaness's most famous and beloved work. *Mysterious Mountain* was not, of course, his second symphony; he had already destroyed at least seven previous ones. Neither was it his opus 132; assigning it that number had been a guess that proved to be too low an estimate and resulted in a number of his earlier works, when they were finally counted, being assigned the same opus number. But the symphony was mysterious sounding, particularly in 1955, and audiences responded to it immediately.

Hovhaness once said that he has loved mountains all his life, telling an interviewer in 1993 that his "main inspiration always came from mountain climbing and nature." In the program notes for *Mysterious Mountain*, he compared mountains to pyramids, calling them symbols "of man's attempt to know God," and "symbolic meeting places between the mundane and spiritual worlds." Later, he said he named the symphony as he did "for that mysterious feeling one has in the mountains."

Hovhaness on Atonality

To me, atonality is against nature.

David Ewen, American Composers, 1982

The reason I like oriental music is that everything has a firm center. All music with a center is tonal. Music without a center is fine for a minute or two, but it soon sounds all the same.

David Ewen, **American Composers,** *1982*

[Serialism] is too artificial for me. I want the melody to be natural, and I like music to be connected with the voice.

Vance Wolverton, **Choral Journal,** *1993*

Musically, *Mysterious Mountain* is its own kind of meeting place, in this case, between East and West, where the melodies and rhythmic practices of the Orient meet the contrapuntal devices and formal designs of Western music. Melodically, Hovhaness writes long, flowing modal melodies with arabesque figurations, using repeated pitches in an almost improvisatory rhythm to create tension. The harmony, when not appearing static, moves in slow modal chords that have their own kind of grandeur. Hovhaness has said that he prefers using the lowered seventh (subtonic) scale degree in his music because it sounds more Eastern than the raised seventh (leading tone) of Western music. And although it reflects a kind of transparent, nondissonant simplicity, *Mysterious Mountain* is not simplistic music. The second movement, for instance, is a double fugue, strictly written in a sophisticated contrapuntal texture that Bach or Handel would have found familiar.

Mysterious Mountain was premiered in Houston on October 31, 1955, with Stokowski conducting. As with most of Hovhaness's works, it met with both immediate acclaim from listeners and acerbic criticism from the establishment. Composer Lou Harrison, a critic for the New York *Herald Tribune* for several years, described the basic problem some composers have with Hovhaness's music as the realization by both the Chromaticists and Americanist camps that here was a composer "whose obviously beautiful and fine music had nothing to do with either camp and was in fact its own very wonderful thing."

Following the success of *Mysterious Mountain*, Hovhaness's music quickly became known and loved throughout the world. A Fulbright Fellowship in 1959 allowed him to tour the Orient, where in India he became the first Western composer asked to participate in the annual music festival in Madras. In Japan, he was met at the airport by the press, appeared on television, and conducted his music with the Tokyo Symphony. A Rockefeller grant in 1962 allowed Hovhaness to return to the Orient, where he studied the ancient court music of Japan and Korea, and conducted the premiere of his Symphony No. 16 for strings and Korean instruments in Seoul.

Between 1936 and 1991 Hovhaness produced sixty-five symphonies, in addition to other works for orchestra. Of these, *And God Created Great Whales*, written in 1970 after he had heard a recording of the songs of humpback whales, and the Symphony No. 50, Op. 360 (*Mount St. Helens*), premiered by the San Jose Symphony in 1984, experienced a degree of popular success seldom encountered in experimental music circles. Hovhaness, who was appointed composer-in-residence to the Seattle Symphony for the 1967-68 season, and has lived there since, said in 1984 that he thought *Mount St. Helens* was his best work. In the fall of 1991, an eightieth-birthday concert for Hovhaness in New York's Carnegie Hall included a performance of *Mysterious Mountain*, as well as the premiere of his Symphony No. 65 (*Artstakh*). In reviewing the concert, *Newsday* said the overall impression of the work was "spiritual, stoic, and elevated."

Hovhaness on Beauty

Things that are very complicated tend to disappear and get lost. Simplicity is difficult, not easy. Beauty is simple. All unnecessary elements are removed—only essence remains.

David Ewen, American Composers, 1982

Today, it's difficult for most people to understand what all the fuss was about in regard to Hovhaness's music. For the most part, the antagonism from fellow composers can probably be attributed to musical politics, and jealousy of his success with the public. What is more difficult to explain is the inspiring quality his music has for the average listener. What other experimental composer, for example, can claim that the owner of a Washington, D.C., record store commissioned a symphony, or that the owner of a California grocery store paid for another work? Even though the majority of Hovhaness's major works are instrumental, most of them are spiritual in nature, and his listeners respond to this in a fundamental way. Somehow, they sense the common ground between East and West, ancient and modern, profound and simple, all of which are put at the service of beauty and made universal by a composer who once told *Down Beat* magazine: "This is not 'intellectual' music, but music of pure feeling."

12

In C

TERRY RILEY

1964

"Music Like None Other On Earth." That was the headline of Alfred Frankenstein's review in the *San Francisco Chronicle*. He was talking about Terry Riley's *In C*, a piece so unlike any previous music that listeners were immediately polarized by it, either drawn in by its grandeur and transcendence, or bored to death. The performance itself, which took place at the San Francisco Tape Music Center in November of 1964, was, from the beginning, a major underground event, drawing poets, dancers, theater people, and many of the city's avant-garde. Composer Morton Subotnick, an organizer of the concert, remembers that Riley showed up wearing "a floppy purple bow tie and orange pants." But that wasn't entirely out of place, considering it was, as Subotnick recalled, "the beginning of the psychedelic dress-up era."

In the atonal, academic climate of the mid-1960s, everything about *In C* was subversive, even the name. Nobody wrote pieces in keys anymore, particularly C major, the most common key of them all. Furthermore, *In C* had a steady pulse, played repeatedly in eighth notes on the top two Cs of the piano, 10,000 repetitions or more if the piece lasted an hour, as it often did. When a performance went all night, as happened in Philadelphia and New York a few years later, the repetitions

Terry Riley. *Photo by Peter Schinzler. © Celestial Harmonies. Used by permission*

of the pulse became too great to count. And if a performance lasted a whole year, as Riley once suggested it could by performing one new pattern each week, the repetitions would be too great to comprehend.

Then there was the score itself, not really a score in the traditional sense, but a collection of fifty-three short fragments or motives, the shortest consisting of only one eighth note, the longest fragment of sixty (the equivalent of four or five measures of music, if *In C* had actually contained any measures). And while these motives were played in order by everyone, from the first to the fifty-third, they were never played together. Instead, each fragment was repeated as many times as an individual performer saw fit. Even the space of silence between the motives was left to the discretion of each performer. The result became "a loose-jointed canon at the unison," to quote Douglas Leedy's notes for the twenty-fifth-anniversary concert CD.

And if all of that wasn't enough to create a controversy, even the performing ensemble itself was a problem. Anybody, even good amateurs, could play the piece, the more the merrier, as long as they played a melody instrument with at least a two-octave range, and could keep in sync with the pulse. Then there was the energy this ad hoc group created, closer to rock or jazz than it was to classical music, as it throbbed and pulsated relentlessly through the repetitions of the patterns, pushed forward by the constant pulse in the piano. With all this, is it any wonder that performances were often described as riveting? *In C*, it seems, was music that depended, not on traditional rules of ensemble playing, but on collective freedom and spontaneous interaction for its success.

Riley on Composing

I started out more as a self-taught musician. I began singing when I was very little . . . . Even before I could talk, I was singing songs off the radio.

Talking Music, 1995

But Terry Riley's *In C*, for all it's uniqueness, is not completely outside the tradition of Western music. Although the pulse remains on C throughout, the music itself slowly shifts pitch centers. Composer David Behrman, who produced the original 1968 recording of the work, described the effect as "a teeming world of groups and subgroups forming, dissolving, and reforming within a [shifting] modal panorama." Douglas Leedy described the effect as "a sparkling, glinting crystal which, as it slowly rotates, changes almost imperceptibly in color from a clear C major to a bright, yet more slowly pulsating, E minor then back to C rather triumphantly, and finally . . . [to] a much more somber and enigmatic G minor." Of course, if the performance lasted all night, it might be 4 A.M. before the modality actually arrived at G. Not only was this music repetitive, but any structural changes that occurred did so at a glacial pace. Is it any wonder that *Glamour* magazine called *In C* "the global village's first ritual symphonic piece"? Music like none other on earth, indeed: Where did this music come from?

Terry Riley was born in 1935 in Colfax, California, a small railroad town in the Sierra Nevada mountains. During high school, he became interested in both the bebop style of jazz played by Charlie Parker and Dizzy Gillespie and the experimental classical music written by Stravinsky and Debussy. Originally, Riley planned a career as a concert pianist, first attending a junior college in Redding, California. But when he transferred to San Francisco State University in 1955, the competition became more intense, and he decided he needed to reconsider his options. At San Francisco State, Riley studied composition with Robert Erickson, and in the process learned, as he said, that "I really enjoyed writing and playing my own music." Although Riley learned Schoenberg's 12-tone technique from Erickson, he described his own music of this period as imitative of the French composers François Poulenc and Darius Milhaud.

In 1958 Riley began graduate classes at the University of California at Berkeley, putting himself through school by playing ragtime piano at the Gold Street Saloon, a place on San Francisco's Barbary Coast that he once described as celebrating "New Year's Eve every night." More important, at Berkeley, Riley met La Monte Young, a fellow composition student who had just written his *Trio for Strings*, a piece of such long, sustained tones and slow moving proportions that it is today considered the first minimalist work. Riley said that he immediately recognized a kinship to Young, and almost from the first believed his "highly evolved" ideas about music were "better than what I was getting from the teachers I came to study with."

After graduating from Berkeley with a degree in composition, Riley moved to Europe, spending the next few years playing piano and saxophone in officers' clubs, touring with a floor show, and, on occasion, participating in happenings and street theater as a self-styled "hippie."

And although he had heard non-Western music at Berkeley, particularly Indian music, two trips to Morocco in the early 1960s gave him his first in-depth exposure to Arabic music—music of florid melodic lines unfolding over static harmonies.

Riley composed very little while in Europe, but he did have the opportunity to work briefly at ORTF (the French National Radio), writing the music for playwright Key Dewey's *The Gift*. With the help of an engineer from the station, Riley created what he called a "time-lag accumulator," essentially two reel-to-reel tape recorders feeding into each other in a loop so that echo effects slowly build into progressively denser textures as the music continues. Riley applied this technique to the composing of *Music for the Gift*, using as source material the sounds of trumpeter Chet Baker's jazz quartet playing Miles Davis's cool jazz classic *So What*. According to Riley, this process of recording the quartet and putting the results through the time-lag accumulator "was when I really started understanding what repetition could do for musical form." According to him, *Music for the Gift* was "the forerunner of *In C*."

Riley on *In C*

When *In C* came, I heard these patterns of the beginning just unravel . . . and I thought, "Boy, what a great idea."

Talking Music, 1995

By the spring of 1964, Riley was again back in San Francisco, supporting himself once more by playing ragtime piano at the Gold Street Saloon. The success in Paris of *Music for the Gift* had shown him the potential of repetitive music, and had made him "want to try a live piece that would have the same effect." The offer of a concert at the Tape Music Center encouraged him to begin composing, and he started trying to create music for instruments similar in style to the tape manipulations he had made from Chet Baker's group. Unfortunately, as he said, "it wasn't working out." Then, one night as he was riding the bus to the saloon, *In C* came into his mind—the structure, the motives, everything—all at once. He said that as soon as he got off work he went home and wrote it all down. He also said he knew immediately that he was onto "something hot," because when he finally saw it come together "it was so simple that I wondered why I hadn't thought of it before." Later, Riley said *In C* was "the piece that opened the door to the world for me." He also said that he never thought about the word *minimalism* when he was writing *In C*. According to him, "I was thinking of some kind of mystical experience. Magic through music."

In 1968, Columbia Records released a recording of *In C*. By that point, Riley had moved to New York, where he reconnected with La Monte Young and performed for a time with Young's Theatre of Eternal Music (replacing John Cale, who was on his way to becoming a rock star). More significantly, it was during this period that Riley stopped writing notated music, preferring instead to concentrate on improvisation. His second album for Columbia, released in 1969, contained *Poppy Nogood and His Phantom Band*, a piece that brought his work with the time-lag accumulator to a close, and *Rainbow in Curved Air*, a work that anticipated his virtuoso keyboard improvisations of the next decade. Riley's performance of these two works in April of 1969 at New York's Electric Circus—"one of the counter-culture's top psychedelic rock clubs," as writer K. Robert Schwarz characterized it—was a clear sign that minimalism was having an impact far beyond anything American experimental music had ever experienced.

Throughout most of the 1970s, Riley immersed himself in Indian music, becoming, along with Young, a disciple of North Indian singer Pandit Pran Nath. In addition to several trips to India, he also taught Indian music at Mills College in Oakland, California. The effect of this new interest on his own music was twofold. First, it changed his approach to melody, and he began to create long flowing melodic lines influenced by, but not imitative of, *raga* style. Second, it awakened his interest in just intonation, a centuries-old form of tuning in which the intervals are tuned mathematically pure, rather than in close approximations as they are in equal temperament. These new elements can be found, to some degree, in most of Riley's music from that period, including *Persian Surgery Dervishes* of 1971 and *Shri Camel* of 1976.

Riley on Minimalism

I think the idea of presenting a certain limited number of musical para-meters so that people can hear them is a valid musical idea, and that's what Minimalism is to me: repetition, long notes, things that people didn't ordinarily build a whole piece out of.

Edward Strickland, **American Composers,** 1991

During the 1980s, Riley again turned to notated music, producing a series of pieces for the Kronos String Quartet. These works, with titles like *Cadenza on the Night Plain* and *Sunrise of the Planetary Dream Collector*, are more lyrical in nature and less concerned with either the layered structuring of motives, (characteristic of his work from the 1960s), or the virtuoso keyboard improvisations of the 1970s. Writer Mark Swed referred to *Salome Dances for Peace*, one of the quartets for the Kronos, as "music of passing landscapes," calling it "a tapestry of seemingly unrelated musics . . . reflecting its composer's passions for jazz blues, North Indian raga, Middle Eastern scales, Minimalist pattern and traditional Western art music; styles never before found together within the framework of a single string quartet." Riley explained this by saying, "I trust the fact that anything that occurs to me is related to whatever occurred to me before."

Others on *In C*

Part of *In C*'s significance is that it granted American music a new start-ing point after the wartime arrival of Stravinsky, Schoenberg, and Hindemith on these shores suffocated the native experimental scene of the '30s.

Kyle Gann, **Village Voice**

Of all Terry Riley's music, however, as varied as it is, none has had the impact of *In C*. Although written more than half a decade after Young's *Trio for Strings*, *In C* became the *de facto* starting point of the minimalist movement in the minds of most listeners. Calling it "an elegant and non-nostalgic return to tonality in art music," Swed said *In C* had "revolutionized music." It certainly provided a change from the oblique and obtuse 12-tone works of the academic serialists, whose music required experts for proper performance. Riley, however, did not lead the minimalist movement much beyond *In C*. As he moved first to improvisation and then to the study of Indian music, minimalism was left to the more systematic and process-oriented styles of composers Steve Reich and Philip Glass. Riley, commenting on the surprise people experience when they learn that he doesn't "feel a musical kinship" with either Reich or Glass, said that, to him, the interrelationship of motives was more important than the minimalist themes. As he put it, "This isn't theoretical; it's the way I hear."

13

Drumming

STEVE REICH

1971

Even today, thirty-five years later, Steve Reich can still recall that moment in the rehearsal when he advised Terry Riley to add a pulse to *In C.* As he remembers, "We couldn't stay together, and, good drummer that I was, I said 'Why don't you have someone just drumming some Cs to keep the beat?'" He concluded, "I think I received more than I gave, but I gave that." What Reich received, in retrospect, was inspiration. And what that inspiration led to was an intense desire on his part to find his own unique way of using repetition as a compositional technique in his own music.

At the time of that rehearsal and the subsequent premiere of *In C,* on which he played a Wurlitzer electric piano, Reich was studying composition at Mills College with Luciano Berio, an Italian composer who was teaching him how to write in the 12-tone style. Born in New York City in 1936, Reich had already graduated from Cornell with a degree in philosophy, and had even studied composition for a time at Juilliard with Vincent Persichetti. The last music he wrote at Juilliard, a piece for string orchestra, was his first 12-tone work. But Reich was also interested in jazz, particularly the bebop sound of drummer Kenny Clarke, and he and his friend Arthur Murphy spent many late nights in the

Steve Reich. *Photo by Nevin Shalit. Used by permission*

New York jazz clubs listening to the likes of Miles Davis, Horace Silver, and Art Blakey. When he got to San Francisco, Reich quickly gravitated toward the Jazz Workshop, and the harmonically static, modal sounds of John Coltrane.

As early as his student days at Juilliard, Reich said he had begun to feel a strong pull between the atonal music his teachers were using as models and the "music built around one tonal center" that moved him emotionally. This dichotomy continued to grow as Reich, now at Mills, grew familiar with Coltrane's music, music that, essentially, built a whole piece out of only one or two chords. Reich said Berio finally told him that if he liked it so much, he should just write tonal music. Later, he said the experience of studying 12-tone music with Berio was valuable, because "it showed me what I had to do—which was to stop writing it." He once characterized his work with Berio as "like being at the scene of the crime with one of the major criminals."

Ironically, it was because of Berio's class that Reich first learned how to turn his attention away from 12-tone music and toward tonality. The composition seminar took a trip to the Ojai festival in 1962, and Reich met composer Gunther Schuller, who suggested he read A. M. Jones's recently published book *Studies in African Music*. Reich said that reading this book awoke his interest in the music of Africa to the point where he began listening to it a great deal. Later, he corresponded with Jones, took several lessons from an Ewe master drummer in New York, and even went to Africa in 1970 to, as he said, "learn some drumming by drumming." Most of Reich's music from the late 1960s on is inconceivable without this African influence.

Reich on His Influences

I heard *The Rite of Spring* at a friend's house, and it was as if somebody had opened a door, saying, "You've been living here all your life, but you haven't seen this room." I just couldn't *believe* that such a thing could exist. It completely changed my idea of what music was about.

*Edward Strickland, **American Composers**, 1991*

An influence closer to home, however, came during the rehearsals of *In C,* when a friend urged Reich to accompany him to San Francisco's Union Square to hear Brother Walter preach his warnings about an impending flood, and the end of the world. Intrigued by the melodic qualities of the preacher's voice, Reich made a tape recording of his sermon, planning to create a speech-based piece of tape music along the lines of a collage. But even though he had worked with tape loops since 1963, Reich credits the experience of preparing *In C* with Riley as the main impetus for the change in direction of the new piece that emerged: *It's Gonna Rain.*

Back in his studio, Reich said he selected the phrase "It's gonna rain" from his recording of Brother Walter, and prepared two identical tape loops, each of which, when played back, would repeat the three-word phrase endlessly. These two loops he then placed on two tape recorders and, after some experimentation, "discovered that the most interesting music of all was made by simply lining the loops up in unison, and letting them slowly shift out of phase with each other," a process that happened every time because no two tape recorders ever run at *exactly* the same speed. Reich called the changes that he heard a "gradual phase shifting process," and said that he slowly came to realize that this process created "an extraordinary form of musical structure." He also said that gradually he began to see phase-shifting "as an extension of the idea of infinite canon or round."

Late in 1966, Reich, now back in New York and still working with tape loops, recorded a short melodic pattern on the piano. From this, he made a tape loop, and then tried to play the same pattern against the loop, as if he were a second tape recorder. To his surprise, he found that while he lacked the technical perfection of the machine, he could approximate the results. The final step was to see if two live pianists could duplicate the effect, and for this Reich called on his friend from Juilliard Arthur Murphy. The piece that resulted from this experiment, *Piano Phase,* was the beginning of a series of live phase pieces that used the gradual phase-shifting process Reich had first discovered in *It's Gonna Rain.*

Basically, phase-shifting, as used by Reich, is an intense, systematic look at a limited amount of musical material. In this sense, the process works like a formula, running the musical material through all of its possible permutations. In the case of *Piano Phase*, both parts begin together, both playing exactly the same thing. But as they play, one part goes out of sync, slowly getting ahead of the other, until they gradually fall into place one beat apart. That is, beat 1 in one piano now corresponds with beat 2 in the other piano. After a while, they slowly shift again, so that beat 1 corresponds to beat 3, and so on, until they make a complete circle and get back together again. Throughout the entire process, the two pianos continue to play the same short pattern they began with, so that the end of the piece, when it finally arrives, sounds exactly like the beginning. In between, however, the music changes with each new shift because the beats never line up in the same way. K. Robert Schwarz, in his book *Minimalists*, observes that with *Piano Phase*, Reich "achieved a systematization worthy of serialism."

Reich on the African Influence on *Drumming*

I didn't write [*Drumming*] because I went to Ghana; I wrote it because I'd been drumming since I was fourteen. Everything African in that piece—12/8, repeating patterns—I'd done in *Piano Phase* and *Violin Phase* back in 1967. Going to Africa was a pat on the back. ·

*Edward Strickland, **American Composers**, 1991*

Between 1965 and the early 1970s, phase-shifting, or phasing, as it commonly came to be called, became Reich's primary method of composing. The culmination of this approach came with *Drumming*, a ninety-minute work Schwarz called "minimalism's first masterpiece." Completed in 1971, *Drumming* is divided into four large sections that are played without pause. Unlike his earlier music, which tends to be for two or more of the same instrument so that the phase shifting can be heard more clearly, the four sections of *Drumming* each use different groups of instruments. The first section calls for four pairs of tuned bongo drums, supplemented with a male voice; the second section uses three marimbas and female voices; the third requires three glockenspiels, augmented by whistling and piccolo; while the fourth combines all of these instruments and voices into a grand finale.

Although the various instruments and voices create a richer sounding texture than that found in any of Reich's previous music, the phase shifting process on which *Drumming* is built is as controlled and austere as it was in *Piano Phase*. And like *Piano Phase*, the basic pattern of *Drumming* is a cycle of twelve beats on which the entire piece—all four sections—is based. For ninety minutes, nothing but the twelve-beat cycle is played. In program notes from 1971, Reich said that in a performance, he and the other musicians "attempt to set aside our individual thoughts and feelings of the moment, and try to focus our minds and bodies clearly on the realization of one continuous musical process."

The actual music of *Drumming* begins with two drummers on bongos, building the basic rhythmic pattern of the piece, one beat at a time. When this is completed, the phasing of the pattern begins, with one drummer slowly moving ahead until the patterns are one beat out of phase with each other. After a complete cycle on bongos, the phasing process is then repeated by the marimbas, then by the glockenspiels, and finally by all the instruments at once. While this is happening, the voices begin to add their own level of complication. Every time a phase shift occurs, it creates a group of resultant patterns. To quote Reich, these resultant patterns are "the impersonal, unintended, psycho-acoustic byproducts of the intended process." In simpler terms, resultant patterns are sub-melodies that occur because of each new realignment of the voices created by the phasing. Every time a phase shift occurs, a new set of resultant patterns emerges.

All of the resultant patterns, what Reich calls sub-melodies, of any one phase shift are present simultaneously within the texture of the piece. What Reich does in *Drumming* is subtly call our attention to some of them by having the voices fade in and out singing them. This can be heard most easily in the marimba section of *Drumming*, where the marimbas are playing the basic pattern out of phase, while the female voices fade in and out singing various resultant patterns. This is a subtle technique, and can be missed on first hearing, because the voices are trying to match the marimba sound, and they never get very loud. A similar method of highlighting the resultant patterns happens with the male voice in the first section, with the piccolo and the whistling in the third, and with all the voices in the fourth.

It is important to realize at this point that *Drumming* is not improvised music, and that the technique required to play this seemingly simple music is enormous. Reich began rehearsing and performing with his own ensemble in 1966. At that time it consisted of three musicians: Reich, Arthur Murphy, and woodwind specialist Jon Gibson. By 1970, it had increased to five. And in 1971, the year *Drumming* was completed, it had grown to thirteen. *Drumming*, first performed at the Museum of Modern Art in New York in December 1971, was the point at which the ensemble changed dramatically. Playing from memory, the group displayed a level of technical perfection and control seldom heard in experimental music. Reich has said that this performance took "almost a year of weekly rehearsals." And when the premiere of *Drumming* was over, Steve Reich and Musicians, as they had taken to calling themselves, received a standing ovation. Shortly after that, they began touring Europe on a regular basis.

Drumming marks the end of Reich's early minimalist phase. In the early 1970s, he studied Indonesian gamelan music in Seattle and Berkeley, and this experience helped redirect his harder percussive sounds toward the softer colors of mallet percussion, eventually resulting in *Music for 18 Musicians*, an hourlong piece many people consider his most significant work. During the 1980s, Reich, who had begun the decade by selling out a performance of his music at Carnegie Hall, began writing for more conventional ensembles. *Tehillim*, a setting of psalm fragments for voices and orchestra, was premiered by the New York Philharmonic in 1982; and *The Desert Music*, a setting of the poetry of William Carlos Williams for chorus and orchestra, was first performed by the Brooklyn Philharmonic in 1984. His most ambitious work of the 1990s, *The Cave*, is a "new kind of music theater" utilizing speechmelodies based on interviews with Jews, Muslims, and Americans, that took Reich and his wife, artist Beryl Korot, five years to record and construct. It was premiered in Vienna in 1993.

But although his music has long since gone in other directions, Steve Reich has remained a hard-core minimalist in the minds of many listeners. As the composer who first systematized and codified repetition, he has become forever linked with the other first-generation minimalists—La Monte Young, Terry Riley, and Philip Glass—and his music, like theirs, is either loved for its gradually unfolding ritualistic qualities, or rejected for its lack of the traditional patterns of tension and release. And in the same way that Riley's *In C* became the *de facto* beginning of minimalism, Steve Reich's *Drumming* became the exemplar of the gradual phase-shifting process, minimalism's most significant compositional technique.

14

I Am Sitting in a Room

ALVIN LUCIER

1969

I am sitting in a room different from the one you are in now.

The date is 1969. The room is the living room of Alvin Lucier's home at 454 High Street in Middletown, Connecticut. He is beginning the recording process for what will become his most famous piece, a work that explores the musical relationship between the disintegration of speech and the reinforcement of the resonant frequencies of the room. For the past several years—first at Brandeis University, then at Connecticut Wesleyan, where he began teaching in 1968—he has been exploring the ways in which the physical characteristics of various environments alter sound, a process he once described as the intruding of the personality of the space onto whatever sounds occur inside it.

I am recording the sound of my speaking voice and I am going to play it back into the room again and again until the resonant frequencies of the room reinforce themselves so that any semblance of my speech, with perhaps the exception of rhythm, is destroyed.

Alvin Lucier. © *Amanda Lucier. Used by permission*

This was not Lucier's first attempt to explore the acoustical properties of sound. Shortly after arriving at Wesleyan he wrote *Chambers*, a piece originally for conch shells, but later extended to include any resonant environment—pots, pans, bottles, bells—that performers could use to produce and alter sounds. He said he wanted to open up our ears to the environment, something he claimed had happened to him while writing the piece. He also said that although it was certainly possible to build an environment that would intentionally alter sounds, he wasn't interested in doing that. As he explained, "I don't want to change anything. I simply want to find out what these environments do to sounds." Lucier referred to this exploratory process as "an extension of what you do when you're a little child at the beach and you put a shell up to your ear and hear the ocean," adding, "I guess I'm trying to help people hold shells up to their ears and listen to the ocean again."

Lucier on Acoustics and Music

I think it's built into my work that I don't succeed very well when I'm thinking in two dimensions; it's always more interesting when I'm thinking in terms of three-dimensional space. It's as if I've completely shifted into another gear. I just can't think of writing a melodic line. Mixing sounds doesn't help much either; that's simply another way of reassembling old materials. Sounds for me have to move not only up and down, but in and out, and across space somewhere; they have to live in space.

Chambers, 1980

I always thought that the world was divided into two kinds of people, poets and practical people, and that while the practical people ran the world, the poets had visions about it. I felt the scientific point of view only skimmed the surface; artists were really the brightest people on earth. Now I realize that there is no difference between science and art.

Chambers, 1980

What you will hear, then, are the natural resonant frequencies of the room articulated by speech.

Previous to writing *I Am Sitting in a Room*, Lucier had also composed *Vespers*, a work in which he used echo guns to help the audience *hear* the acoustical characteristics of an enclosed space. In *Vespers*, which was named for a North American bat of the *Vespertillionidae* family, the performance begins with the musicians spread throughout the performing area; sometimes, as in New York's Steinway Hall, it even began out on the street. The musicians are either blindfolded, or the space is dimly lit and they wear dark glasses. The space itself is relatively empty.

The performers are equipped with handheld echolocation devices. Their task is to orient themselves acoustically by taking readings of the space. In the process of doing this, they create interesting rhythms by changing the angle of reflection of the echo clicks, and they produce and move multiple echoes to different locations within the space. In the score, Lucier tells his performers to "move as non-human migrators, artificial gatherers of information, or slow ceremonial dancers." He once said that, with *Vespers*, he wanted "to make the space be the interesting thing," not the personalities of the composer or the performers. According to him, "What goes out into space has to be neutral" so that the acoustical phenomena can be experienced more clearly. In *Vespers*, as in many of Lucier's pieces, "the space and the situation take over."

I regard this activity not so much as a demonstration of a physical fact, but more as a way to smooth out any irregularities my speech might have.

The actual recording of *I Am Sitting in a Room* required little in the way of sophisticated electronic equipment. A microphone, two reel-to-reel tape recorders, an amplifier, and a loudspeaker were all that were needed. What Lucier did was to read the text (given above in italics), and record it on one of the tape recorders. This first-generation recording of his voice he then played back into the room through the loudspeaker, and recorded that with the microphone and the second tape recorder. This second-generation tape he then played through the speaker and into the room again, simultaneously recording a third generation of his voice with the other tape recorder. He continued in this way until he had created fifteen generations of his taped voice reading the text.

It is important to realize, at this point, what the actual compositional process consisted of. The speech was not dubbed from one recorder to another (a process that would result in a gradual degeneration of the tape from copy to copy), but rather played back into the space. This means that the signal was not only processed electronically, but processed acoustically as well. Lucier has said that he had to use tape to create *I Am Sitting in a Room* because it was the only way in which he could recycle sounds into space and have the results be accessible. Tape, then, wasn't a medium in which to compose, as it was for some, but a conveyor—a means to record and play back the sounds in chronological order.

For someone listening to *I Am Sitting in a Room* for the first time, the results can be startling. In the earliest generations of the tape, both Lucier's voice and the text are clear and audible, with any changes sounding as if they are produced by EQ and echo, more so than by the acoustical properties of the room. Somewhere in the middle generations, however, the words begin to blur, making parts of the text difficult to understand. And in their place, pitched drones appear, the result of the reinforcement of particular frequencies by the architecture of the space. By the final generations of the tape, the text is no longer discernible, and Lucier's voice becomes a wordless melody, singing over a rich complex of slowly moving drones, all articulated by the remnants of speech rhythm and Lucier's slight stutter.

Technically, the reason this effect happens as it does is that the space inside a room acts as a filter, eliminating some frequencies and reinforcing others. If the shape of the room is compatible with the wavelength of a particular sound that is played into it, that sound will be amplified as it is reflected from the walls. If, on the other hand, the wavelength is incompatible and doesn't "fit" the room, the sound will grow gradually weaker and disappear as it reflects out of phase with itself, thus canceling itself out. Lucier calls this process "a form of amplification by repetition," and says that "thinking of sounds as measurable wavelengths . . . has changed my whole idea of music from a metaphor to a fact and, in a real way, has connected me to architecture." He also said that his primary interest was not so much scientific, as it was "in opening that secret door to the sound situation that you experience in a room."

Musically, more is happening in *I Am Sitting in a Room* than it may seem on the surface. To begin, there is the repetitive process of the tape recording and the talking, a compositional form akin to the repetitive processes of minimalism. Then, there are the extraordinary results this process yields. Furthermore, even though the form is repetitive, each room produces different results, and each listener hears something different every time. This difference has to do with locating that climactic moment during which Lucier's speech goes from intelligible to unintelligible, and is transformed into pure sound. Lucier describes this moment as going "from words to music," and says that "it seems to operate on its own set of rules," adding, "It's very mysterious."

Lucier on *I Am Sitting in a Room*

My first impulse was to use various musical instruments playing a wide variety of sounds, but I tossed that idea out because it felt too "composerly." Instead I decided to use speech; it's common to just about everybody and is a marvelous sound source.

Chambers, 1980

I don't want what goes into the space to be too poetic. I want it to be plain so that the space becomes audible without distractions; that's why I decided to describe the recording process so that the audience could more easily understand what's going on.

Chambers, 1980

Every room has its own melody, hiding there until it is made audible.

Chambers, 1980

For many listeners, Lucier's work may seem closer to a scientific experiment than to a piece of music. But he says that he is not a scientist and that he was brought up to believe that his interests in the world were purely artistic, and that scientific endeavors were beyond him. As he put it, "I never thought I could fix anything." Certainly, his training was neither experimental nor scientific. Born in New Hampshire in 1931, Lucier attended Yale University, where he studied composition with Quincy Porter, and Brandeis, where he studied with Arthur Berger. He remembers that during the time he spent at Yale, the name of Charles Ives was rarely mentioned, "and John Cage was considered a clown." In 1959, and again in 1960, he attended the Tanglewood Summer Festival, studying orchestration with Aaron Copland and composition with Lukas Foss.

Later in 1960, he went to Italy on a Fulbright, studying first in Venice, then in Rome. He said that it was while living in Italy that he realized he was "merely copying European models," adding that he knew that if he "were going to make music of any value whatsoever, I had better strike out on my own."

The piece in which Lucier first struck out on his own—written in 1965 after he was back in Massachusetts and teaching at Brandeis—was *Music for Solo Performer*, a work for enormously amplified brain waves and percussion. Lucier had made the acquaintance of Edmond Dewan, a physicist on the Brandeis faculty working on brain-wave research for the Air Force. Dewan had an apparatus that measured alpha activity in the brain, and he offered it to Lucier to use artistically. Lucier, who said he had lost confidence in the musics of his education by that point and "felt the need for a new idea," approached the challenge with "a ready and open mind." The result was a piece—the first of its kind—using amplified alpha waves panned through sixteen channels of sound to excite percussion instruments and make them speak. Lucier said he got the idea to couple the loudspeakers to percussion instruments by watching the high energy bursts of alpha "come bumping through the loudspeakers," making the grille cloth vibrate. For the first performance at the Rose Art Museum at Brandeis in 1965, Lucier sat motionless, generating alpha. His assistant, who panned the alpha waves through the various channels and into the loudspeakers, was John Cage. Cage was there to give a concert, and had insisted that Lucier participate with a piece of his own.

From these early beginnings, Lucier continued to explore acoustical ephemera, fashioning, in the words of composer and writer Daniel Wolf, "a music that demands an altered attention." For his first sound installation, created in 1977, Lucier strung a long metal wire the length of a room, attaching both ends to an audio oscillator. Across the wire he placed a horseshoe magnet, causing the wire to vibrate because of the interaction between the current in the wire and the magnetic field placed across it. Lucier said he got the idea for the piece in the acoustics lab at Wesleyan. Acknowledging that "there is little or no musical language at the input stage" of *Music on a Long Thin Wire*, as he named it, he characterized the result as "strands of pure tones" creating a steady-state environment in which fluctuations inherent in the system can be clearly perceived, adding, "I think of them as *canti firmi*, out of which the music flows."

More recently, Lucier was asked by pianist Aki Takahashi to write an arrangement of a Beatles song for a compilation album she was making for Toshiba-EMI. Agreeing to do it, but refusing to pick the song, Lucier asked her to choose. She selected "Strawberry Fields Forever" because she said the line "Nothing is real" reminded her of Lucier's music. Lucier said at first he thought of composing a piece similar in style to *I Am Sitting in a Room*, but his experiments with playing the song on a piano through a digital delay didn't interest him at all. Finally, he decided to play the sounds into a teapot, allowing the resonances of the pot to reinforce certain pitches of the song. The resulting composition, *Nothing Is Real (Strawberry Fields Forever)*, completed in 1991, consists of the pianist playing fragments of the melody, some notes of which are sustained as clusters, and recording it on tape. The tape is then played back through a small loudspeaker hidden inside the teapot. While the tape is being played back, the lid of the pot is raised and lowered, altering the resonant characteristics of the pot.

Of all the pieces Lucier has written that explore the acoustics of sound, none is more widely recognized than *I Am Sitting in a Room*. When it was premiered at New York's Guggenheim Museum in 1970, the sounds were accompanied by images created by the visual artist Mary Lucier, his wife at the time. What she did was to prepare a visual analog to the compositional process by subjecting a Polaroid snapshot to a similar reproductive plan. The snapshot she used was of the chair that Lucier sat in when he made the original recording. As she copied the original, then copied the copy, and copied that copy, slight errors in size crept in. The result was that the image enlarged slightly and began to move off the picture. In a similar way, Lucier's presence in his music is both larger than life, and slightly out of the picture. Unlike most composers, he does not try to interject his personality into either the performing space or his manipulation of it. Rather, he is content to make audible that which is normally inaudible, allowing the various acoustical phenomena to *speak* for themselves. As he once said, "Most of my pieces are built on physical or acoustical principles that you can talk about—alpha waves, echoes, resonances, things of that kind. But they become interesting, for me anyway, when you can't talk about them anymore."

15

4th String Quartet
Amazing Grace

BEN JOHNSTON

1973

Many people are surprised to learn that the piano, as well as all other Western instruments of fixed pitch, isn't really in tune acoustically. This pitch discrepancy isn't great—in fact, it's "damn close," to quote composer Ben Johnston—but it isn't exact. Equal temperament, the dominant Western tuning system for more than two centuries, has the advantage of allowing instruments like the piano to be played in all keys without the necessity of retuning, but it does this at the expense of acoustically pure intervals. The perfect fifths are slightly flat, the major thirds are too wide. And for composers like Ben Johnston, who specialize in getting their music in tune, this makes all the difference in the world. To him, most of the music we hear in the course of our daily lives is slightly out of tune.

In the earliest examples of western European art music, written before fixed-pitch instruments like the harpsichord and the piano were invented, tuning was a simpler matter. Most instrumentalists and all singers performed in just intonation. Just intonation is a tuning system in which all the intervals of the scale are tuned in perfect mathematical

Ben Johnston.

relationships to each other. This means that the two pitches of an octave vibrate at a ratio of exactly 2:1, the upper note vibrating twice as fast as the lower. Likewise, a perfect fifth vibrates at the exact ratio of 3:2; a perfect fourth at exactly 4:3; and a major second at precisely 9:8. But although just intonation is wonderfully "in tune," it has a major flaw: it works with only one key at a time. If, for instance, the piano is tuned in the key of C major in just intonation, it is perfectly in tune for that key, but hopelessly out of tune for all other keys. So if a piece of music were to modulate to a different key, the piano would need to be retuned. Obviously, almost none of the music of the Classic and Romantic eras, with their emphasis on key relationships and modulation, could have been written in this tuning.

As fixed-pitch instruments became more prominent—first the organ, then the harpsichord, and finally the piano—this characteristic of just intonation became an increasing problem. As it did so, various solutions, called temperaments, were introduced. Basically, a temperament is a slight altering of the acoustically pure intervals of just intonation, in order to create a set of usable keys for fixed-pitch instruments. In the early 1800s, meantone temperament became popular because it made seven keys available without the necessity of retuning. But as composers continued to explore new key relationships, along with more chromatic melodies and harmonies, it too became inadequate. So by the mid-1800s, most musicians had adopted equal temperament. The advantage of equal temperament is that it is usable in all keys. The disadvantage is that only the octave (2:1) is really in tune; all other intervals are adjusted slightly and thus are not acoustically pure.

For most composers (and listeners), this trade-off is not a problem. They are willing to accept the inherent out-of-tuneness, which is not that great to begin with, in favor of the chromatic latitude offered by equal temperament. But not all composers agree, Ben Johnston among them. He argues that this replacement of simple vibrating ratios with more complex ones creates a music that has no color. For him, music written in equal temperament contains only varying shades of gray, similar, as he says, to watching color movies on a black-and-white TV. To his ear, consonance and dissonance in music is a result of the low or high vibrating ratios of the intervals, and beauty in music is created by the interplay between these low-ratio and high-ratio vibrations, an experience not possible in equal temperament. To the people who protest that they can't hear such minute distinctions, Johnston responds, "Yes you can; you just have to know what to listen for." He continues the television metaphor by adding, "Listening to music in equal temperament is like watching a television that is slightly out of focus. You don't know it's a problem unless someone adjusts it for you. Then you say, 'Oh, now I see.'" According to him, *anyone* can hear the difference when it's pointed out to them.

Ben Johnston said he first became aware that music was out of tune when he was eleven years old, but that he had little opportunity to explore the issue until he began reading about acoustics as a freshman in college during World War II. Later, in graduate school at the Cincinnati Conservatory in 1950, a musicologist on the faculty gave him Harry Partch's recently published book *Genesis of a Music*, in which Partch discusses the history of tuning, and talks about the theoretical basis of his own music, much of which is written in a 43-note scale. Johnston was so taken with Partch's ideas that he immediately wrote to him, and within a year had moved to California to become Partch's apprentice. Johnston and his wife, Betty, can be heard on some of Partch's earliest 78 r.p.m. recordings, playing such instruments as the kithara and the diamond and bass marimbas, instruments that Partch had invented in order to play his music. Unfortunately, Partch's health deteriorated quickly, and within six months Johnston had left his apprenticeship and had entered Mills College, where he continued to study composition with French composer Darius Milhaud. By the fall of 1951, Johnston was teaching at the University of Illinois, a job he held until his retirement in 1983.

Johnston on Tuning and Temperament

In a way, intellectually, temperament is the big enemy. What is it? It's a lie. It's a pretense. It's close enough for jazz, only it isn't jazz that it's close enough for. It's close enough for classical music.

Talking Music, 1995

Look at it from a Platonic or from a Confucian point of view: music causes psychological results, political results, and social results. Look at the situation of rock music in the world today. It's a cause; it's not simply a passive reflection.

Talking Music, 1995

I think that the symbolism in music is appreciated and understood by every human being, on some level or other, even down to the vibrations per second. And I think that I don't want to deal, as an artist, with those adulterated symbols, because I think, to some extent, they're poisonous. And I think that one of the things that's wrong with our society is that instead of aiming at the best or at the purest, we're aiming at something a whole lot more pragmatic—what's convenient, what's going to work—and that may, indeed, involve a whole lot of consequences.

Talking Music, 1995

Although Harry Partch made a profound impact on Johnston's thinking as a composer, he was not the only significant influence on his work. During Johnston's second year at Illinois, John Cage gave a lecture on composing with chance. From this initial encounter, Cage invited Johnston to study with him in New York, and Johnston spent the summer of 1952 there helping Cage and composer Earle Brown prepare Cage's electronic work *William's Mix*. Toward the end of the decade, Johnston returned to New York on a Guggenheim Fellowship to work at the Columbia-Princeton Electronic Music Center on the application of electronic instruments to microtonal music, but problems with his access to the equipment resulted in his studying with Cage instead. And even though Cage did not directly affect Johnston's work with microtonal music, he was responsible, in large part, for Johnston's attitude about experimentation. And both Cage and Partch influenced Johnston's willingness, and single-mindedness, to plot his own course, a course even further from the mainstream, as it turned out, than either of them.

Johnston on Cage and Partch

I was really taken with him [Cage]. I thought he was the "Real McCoy"—the first person I had met, other than Harry Partch, who I thought was a real original.

Talking Music, 1995

When I was a Boy Scout, for God's sake, going for Life Scout—doing a music merit badge—I had to do a shtick on American music, and the only people who interested me were Ives and Ruggles and those people. They were the only ones with any guts . . . with any profile. So when I encountered Partch I recognized this animal. And Cage.

Talking Music, 1995

Although early in his career Johnston experimented with a variety of compositional styles, including serialism, neoclassicism, and chance, his real interests lay in tuning and intonation, and his work slowly began to focus in that direction. Furthermore, his difficulties at the Columbia-Princeton studio had convinced him that electronic instruments were not suitable for his purposes, while his apprenticeship with Partch had taught him that he could never hope to succeed at building his own instruments, as Partch had done. His only recourse, he came to believe, was to return to writing microtonal music for traditional instruments, even though he knew it would mean working in relative isolation and obscurity until the worth of his unorthodox ideas was more widely appreciated and understood.

While Ben Johnston has written microtonal music for a wide variety of traditional instruments, including the piano (which he retunes), he is best known for a series of ten microtonal string quartets that he began in the early 1960s. Of these, his *String Quartet No. 4*, a set of nine variations on the hymn tune "Amazing Grace," is his most popular work. Written in 1973, it represents a significant change in his compositional style. While the Second and Third Quartets apply serial techniques to a 53-tone scale, the Fourth Quartet represents an abandonment of serialism, and a return to his own particular brand of microtonal tonality. And although Johnston's Fourth Quartet is an amazingly complex work in which the same ratios that govern pitch are applied to the control of rhythmic and tempo relationships as well, the complexity develops gradually, and in a somewhat recognizable fashion. This, plus the fact that the form of the work is a theme and variations based on a hymn tune known to almost everyone, makes it an ideal first choice for those of us trying to understand what microtonal composers really hear when they write microtonal music.

By the late 1960s, Johnston's ideas on tuning had developed into a complicated, but logical, system of extended just intonation. In general terms, extended just intonation is an expansion of traditional just tuning. The purpose is to create an extended matrix of microtonal pitches, inplied, but not found in the original system. Basically, what this means is that in extended just intonation, a few precisely tuned intervals are chosen, from which the many pitches of a microtonal scale are then generated. Johnston, by this point, had found it necessary to limit the number of generative intervals he used, in order to keep the vast number of microtonal pitches they created down to a workable number. In Johnston's case, he uses the unison, octave, perfect fifth, major third, natural seventh, and sometimes the natural eleventh and thirteenth as generative tones. By tuning acoustically pure intervals above and below these tones, he is able to create a matrix of microtonal pitches, all of which are related to each other in an acoustically pure way. From this matrix of pitches, he can then extract the intervals and scale patterns with which he wants to work. The purpose of so many tones per octave is to make available a wide variety of intervals, some of which vibrate with the clarity and beauty of low-ratio intervals, others of which exhibit the tension-filled dissonances of high-ratio vibrations.

Johnston begins his Fourth Quartet with the statement of the hymn tune "Amazing Grace" in its traditional sixteen-bar version, written in a Pythagorean pentatonic tuning. The pentatonic scale is a 5-note scale associated with much of the world's folk music, and "Amazing Grace" has always been written in that scale. Johnston derives the Pythagorean version of this scale by tuning two consecutive perfect fifths (3:2) up and down from the pitch A. He then harmonizes the melody with intervals of fourths and fifths in a three-part setting for two violins and viola. In the first variation, he begins to use rhythms of three against two. This is the rhythmic equivalent of his vertical use of fourths and fifths in the harmony. In Variation 2, he applies this proportion to each member of the quartet by relating them to each other in a 3:2 relationship. This results in the simultaneous time signatures of 2/4, 6/8, and 9/16. With Variation 3, Johnston expands the group of intervals treated as consonant to include major and minor thirds and major and minor sixths, resulting in the formation of a 7-tone just major scale.

The matrix of microtonal pitch possibilities increases with Variation 4, where Johnston introduces intervals created from the natural seventh. These 7th-partial intervals allow the creation of a 12-tone major scale, similar in sound to the blues scale. It is worth noting in this regard that Variation 4 is twelve bars long, rather than sixteen, as are the other variations. In Variations 5 and 6, Johnston continues to work with 7th-partial intervals. In Variation 6 he sets an inversion of the hymn tune in a 12-tone minor scale, a scale formed by internally inverting the 12-tone major scale. Variation 7 combines these two scales to form a 22-tone major-minor scale. Variation 8 contains the most complex pitch usage of the quartet, employing material based on both the 12-tone major scale and the 22-tone major-minor scale. In Variation 9, Johnston begins in 12-tone major, but by the end, the 7-tone major scale predominates. The final cadence of the quartet is a subdominant seventh chord, separated by a pause from the tonic chord, played without a third.

But how much of this can really be heard by someone listening to microtonal music for the first time? Surprisingly, quite a lot. Certainly, the gradual introduction of prime generative integers, and the enlarged pitch matrix this creates can be heard, as can the changing levels of consonance and dissonance that it creates. And the movement from a 5-tone pentatonic scale, to a 7-tone just major scale, to a 12-tone major, then a 12-tone minor, and finally a 22-tone major-minor scale (the most complicated scale Johnston uses in the Fourth Quartet), while unusual, is sufficiently different to be noticeable on first hearing. The trick is not to try to hear every minute pitch inflection at once, but instead to listen for areas of perfect intonation counterbalanced with points of intervallic dissonance and tension. Johnston says that he hears a "chain of relationships" produced by, and unique to, each scale. It is also possible to listen for the "color" of the various intervals, many of which seem more vivid than they do in music written in equal temperament. More problematic on first hearing is Johnston's rhythmic mirroring of pitch proportions, a technique closer in style to medieval and Renaissance composers than it is to Johnston's contemporaries, but this too can be heard as a form of ever expanding rhythmic complexity. And although trying to find one's place in a piece of microtonal music can be a daunting first experience, keep in mind that, in Johnston's case, he is trying to create a wider range of intervallic relationships than is possible in equal temperament, and that he is doing this in order to perfect the tuning.

Ben Johnston's Fourth Quartet was originally commissioned by the Fine Arts Quartet, and was premiered by them on April 21, 1974, at Carnegie Recital Hall in New York. Writing about a later performance by the Concord Quartet for the *New York Times*, critic John Rockwell characterized the sound as "flowing and shifting as the intonation changes hues." He went on to say that the Quartet was "almost corny, but manages to stop short of that and be simply beautiful instead." Theorist Randall Shinn, writing in *Perspectives of New Music* in 1977, focused on the many contrasts between innovation and tradition found in the Fourth Quartet. He points out that while the work is a traditional theme and variation on a simple, well-known hymn tune, it is written with a fluctuating proportional complexity "so novel as to be almost unprecedented." He also says that while the string quartet is a traditional combination of instruments treated in a conservative way by Johnston, the demands he makes upon the players are extraordinary. Shinn concludes that "whatever the reason, his [Johnston's] music seems to function in a way the ear is prone to comprehend."

Johnston on His Fourth Quartet

I think listeners hear a process of gradual involvement and gradual densification. . . . And, also, they might be aware that it's getting more elaborate, like a plant. You can start a tree from the ground, you know; you're looking at the trunk; then you're looking at branches; finally, you're looking at all the little filaments of the leaves, and all the detail. Well, as we grow through the Fourth Quartet, it's like we're ascending that tree, and getting out onto the branches.

unpublished interview with the author, 1997

And that, of course, is what Johnston has been after all along: aural comprehension by the average listener. Even in the midst of such pitch and rhythmic complexity, Ben Johnston writes music for the ear, trying not to confuse, but to clarify. The many pitches of his microtonal universe are put at the service of perfect intonation. His goal is to create music that reaches each listener at the fundamental level of vibration. And for him, this is not a whim, but a necessity. As he says, "I'm inclined toward the view, like Plato and Confucius, where music has a causative effect on human relationships." As he sees it, the kind of music people are exposed to "molds, changes, and makes them different." And even though it may at first seem contradictory, given the complexity of his music, Johnston believes that music is not simply an intellectual exercise, but a physical response to sound. For Ben Johnston, any music that pretends to be in tune when it isn't, is a bad moral model.

16

Einstein on the Beach

PHILIP GLASS

1976

When Philip Glass arrived in Paris in 1963 at the age of twenty-six, he was already well on the way to establishing himself as a composer. Born in Baltimore in 1937, he had taken flute lessons as a child at the Peabody Conservatory; attended the University of Chicago while still a teenager; and studied composition at Juilliard for five years with William Bergsma and Vincent Persichetti, completing some seventy student pieces, a few of which were published. He had even served two years as a Ford Foundation composer in the Pittsburgh public schools, writing marches for the school band and songs for the chorus, most of it in a style reminiscent of Aaron Copland. But by the time he returned to New York three years later, all of this groundwork had been abandoned. Instead, his time in Paris had been spent rebuilding his musical technique from the ground up, learning to *hear* music in a way previously unimaginable to him, and laying the foundation for a new steady-state, repetitive music that would become the most popular classical music of the last quarter of the twentieth century. The two people responsible for this fundamental change of heart were Nadia Boulanger, the composition teacher of Copland and generations of other American composers after

Phillip Glass. *Corbis-Bettmann*

him, and Ravi Shankar, the Indian sitar virtuoso who popularized Indian classical music in the West.

Glass went to Paris on a Fulbright fellowship specifically to study with Boulanger. He said he knew he needed a more solid technique than the one he had acquired, and he had chosen Boulanger as his teacher because a successful musician he knew and admired at Juilliard had studied with her. She was now seventy-five years old. Once lessons began, Boulanger made Glass start over again from the beginning: "counterpoint, solfege, and analysis, all day long," as he later characterized it. Glass said that Boulanger was such "an incomparable model of discipline and dedication" that he had had to work continually just to keep up with her expectations. He also said it took a certain courage on his part to submit himself to that kind of rigor, as he was already in his mid-twenties and had a master's degree from Juilliard. But in the end, Glass said he came away with "a very different grasp of music," one focused on the art of hearing, and based on the acquisition of skills and techniques, rather than a mere learning of the rules. Later, saying there was nothing easy that couldn't be made more difficult by Boulanger and her assistant, Glass confided that even after he became famous and returned to Paris years later to play with his ensemble, he still had a recurring fear that Boulanger would be there, sitting in the front row.

Glass on Composing

Musicians have something like a calling, a religious calling. It's a vocation. I think it happens before we know it's going to happen. At a certain point you realize that's the only thing you can take seriously.

Talking Music, 1995

I have very good habits. I guess I learned them from Boulanger. I usually get up at six and work until noon, except the days when I'm on the road. The afternoons I spend in the studio.

Talking Music, 1995

During his second year in Paris, Glass met Ravi Shankar. Shankar had been engaged to write the music for Conrad Rooks's film

Chappaqua, and someone was needed to transcribe his music into Western notation so the French musicians could read it. Glass said that while he found the melodic aspects of Indian music fascinating, what really attracted him was the rhythm, and how it could be used to develop the overall structure of a piece. As he worked on the transcriptions with Shankar and his tabla player, Allah Rakha, he slowly began to understand how Indian musicians strung together small rhythmic cells into larger time values, and then even larger sections—an additive process fundamentally different from the Western practice of *dividing* time into smaller and smaller increments. Glass said he found this revelation, which he once characterized as "like wheels inside of wheels, everything going at the same time and always changing," to be so powerful that he immediately began trying to use it in his own work. And while still in Paris, he wrote his first piece of music using repetition and additive processes. The music, for a production of Samuel Beckett's *Play*, was for two soprano saxophones, each playing two notes that pulsed in alternating patterns; music Glass described as "very static . . . [but] full of rhythmic variety."

If the new techniques Glass learned from Boulanger, along with the new insights he gained from Indian classical music represented the beginnings of a new musical language for him, his contact with experimental theater offered him a continuing opportunity to test his ideas out. The American theater company that had staged Beckett's *Play* in Paris became known, upon its return to New York in 1967, as Mabou Mines; Glass, who was then married to one of its members, began a long collaboration with them as an unofficial composer-in-residence, creating the music for some twelve productions over the next twenty years. Equally important to the development of his ideas was the performing group he assembled shortly after returning to New York. He said he put it together because he knew that if his new style of music was going to be played, he would have to be the one to play it. His group, which he called the Philip Glass Ensemble, consisted of electric pianos and organs (picked for their portability), an amplified soprano voice, and three amplified woodwind players, doubling primarily on saxophones and flutes. He added a sound designer and mixer in 1970. The music he wrote for his group was rhythmic, repetitive, consonant, fast, and loud.

To someone with only a casual knowledge of Philip Glass's work during this period of the mid-1970s, it might seem that he was developing along two parallel, but totally separate, paths. But he didn't see it this way. Pointing out that his musical language was similar for both situations, Glass said that, for him, "theater became the catalyst for musical innovation, and the Ensemble gave me both the instrument and the opportunity to develop ideas apart from the practical, and more circumscribed, demands of the theater itself." The two came together when Glass first saw Robert Wilson's work in experimental theater, attending an all-night performance of *The Life and Times of Josef Stalin* at the Brooklyn Academy of Music in 1973. Within a year of this first encounter, Glass and Wilson were meeting regularly over lunch, exploring mutual interests, and discussing projects they might do together. It was from these meetings that the major themes and structures of *Einstein on the Beach* came to be.

Glass on Theater

My [early] work in the theater had much more to do with Cage and Cunningham than with any of the musicians I knew.

Talking Music, 1995

The theater has always been a haven for progressive music .... The dramatic needs of a work can often justify experiments that you could never get away with in a concert hall.

Talking Music, 1995

During those early meetings of 1974, Wilson and Glass decided on most of the important features of *Einstein on the Beach*. They chose a running time of four hours, although, in reality, it proved to be closer to five. They determined the three visual themes: a Train, a Trial, and a Field with Spaceship. And they decided that the opera would be divided into four acts of nine scenes, the acts surrounded and separated by five short interludes they began calling Knee Plays. They also concluded that no theater or opera company would want to produce a work such as the one they envisioned, and that they would have to raise the money and do it themselves. Glass said that during those meetings it never occurred to either of them that *Einstein on the Beach* would have an actual story or conventional plot. Instead, it was always a "portrait" opera, developed through poetic license, with any "story" involved supplied by the imaginations of the audience. For Glass, "It hardly mattered what you thought *Einstein on the Beach* might 'mean.'"

By the time Glass began to compose the music, Wilson's sketchbook for the production was almost complete. Beginning in the spring of 1975, Glass said the music came quickly, and the score was finished by November. He also said he wrote the scenes in order, except for the Knee Plays, which he composed last. The music for *Einstein on the Beach* is written for four principal actors, a chamber choir of twelve singers (doubling when possible as dancers and actors), a solo violinist dressed as Albert Einstein, and the Philip Glass Ensemble.

Throughout the opera, Glass uses additive and cyclic processes to create the actual music. The additive process consists of repeating a short group of, say, six notes, followed by a repeated group of seven notes, then a repeated group of eight, then nine, then ten, then nine, then eight, and so on. Glass called this one of those simple ideas "that can quickly lead to very complicated procedures." The cyclic process he created "by superimposing two different rhythmic patterns of different lengths." By repeating each pattern enough times, they eventually arrive back at their starting points together, making one complete cycle. These two processes could also be combined. As Glass told an interviewer for *Contemporary Keyboard* in 1981, "What regularly happens in my music is that I'll set up a recurring meter of three in one hand and a cycle of meters in the other, so that against the three you'll have nine, eight, six, five, four, three, four, five, six, eight, nine, and twelve all worked out so that they fit the basic cycle of three but nevertheless require a good rhythmic feeling to carry them off."

By using these additive and cyclic processes, separately and in combination, Glass is able to write music of constant change inside a texture that appears repetitive and static. And because the basic rhythmic cells of his music constantly vary, it is difficult for the singers to remember the patterns and keep their place in the score. Glass said this was why he began to use solfège syllables and numbers during the rehearsals of *Einstein on the Beach*. Originally an aid to memorization, these "lyrics"—*do-re-mi*, and *one-two-three*—eventually became the sung vocal text of the opera. The spoken texts were contributed by several people, including Christopher Knowles, a fourteen-year-old neurologically impaired boy whom Wilson had discovered, who was capable, according to Glass, "of writing things of startling originality"; Lucinda Childs, who also choreographed her own dance solos in the first Train scene; and Samuel M. Johnson, who appeared as the Judge in the Trial scenes and the Bus Driver in the last Knee Play.

Einstein on the Beach was premiered at the Avignon Festival in France in August of 1976. Glass said that it was clear from the beginning that it was *the* event of the festival, with many in the audience returning as often as they could. When the tickets were gone, people began sneaking into the theater, and the opera quickly gained a cult following. According to Glass, "These kinds of intense, almost fanatical, followers appeared again and again throughout Europe over the next four months," as the tour moved from France through Italy, Germany, Yugoslavia, Holland, and Belgium, a six-country tour of over thirty performances.

As the tour wound its way through Europe, performing in such established opera houses as the Opera Comique in Paris, La Fenice in Venice, and La Monnaie in Brussels, plans began to take shape for an American premiere at the prestigious Metropolitan Opera House in New York in November 1976. Like other performing spaces, the house was usually dark on Sunday nights, and could be rented for special occasions. The Met is a 4,000-seat house, and Glass admitted to being concerned during the tour that it might be half empty for the American performance. After all, the largest crowd he had ever attracted to a performance of his music in New York was some 1,200 to Town Hall for a concert of *Music in Twelve Parts* in 1974. But not only did the first night at the Met sell out, so did the second performance on the following Sunday night. Glass said he had trouble even getting tickets for his own family, who were coming from Baltimore. Clive Barnes, writing for the *New York Times*, called the production "bizarre, occasionally boring, yet always intermittently beautiful." Of Glass's music he said, "It is almost more monotonous than Bach's . . . and, more important, at times almost as interesting."

Philip Glass said his life didn't change all that much after *Einstein on the Beach* played the Met. In fact, he returned to driving a taxi—his day job of the past few years—and, later, he loved to tell the story about the woman who, on entering his cab and seeing his license, asked him if he knew he had the same name as a famous composer. But of course Glass's life did change, and change dramatically. After the success of *Einstein on the Beach*, Glass wrote two more portrait operas: *Satyagraha*, based on Gandhi's early years in South Africa, and premiered by the Netherlands Opera in 1980; and *Akhnaten*, based on a pharaoh of fifteenth-century B.C.E. Egypt who was the first to introduce monotheism as a state religion. Commissioned by the Stuttgart State Opera, *Akhnaten* was premiered by them in 1984. Writer K. Robert Schwarz observed that with the completion of his trilogy of portrait operas, "Philip Glass was now the best-known and most sought-after living composer."

The 1980s were a period of extraordinary success and recognition for Philip Glass. He began the decade by being named *Musical America*'s "Musician of the Month" in April of 1979. By 1985, he was their "Musician of the Year," an honor previously given only to Igor Stravinsky and Benjamin Britten. In 1982, he became only the third composer in history to sign an exclusive recording contract with CBS Masterworks—the other two were Stravinsky and Copland—and within four years his first album for them, *Glassworks*, sold more than 175,000 copies. And in 1988, twenty-two years after *Einstein on the Beach* first played the Met, Philip Glass received a commission from the Metropolitan Opera to write a work commemorating the 500th anniversary of the discovery of America by Columbus. The premiere of this opera, *The Voyage*, on Columbus Day 1992, was heard not only by sold-out houses at the Met, but by a worldwide radio audience as well. As Glass once said, "My intention was always to look for a broader public." Having now found one, history may well bestow on Philip Glass the title "Musician of the Decade. "

17

Perfect Lives

ROBERT ASHLEY

1983

Reportedly, there was a Robert Ashley in the audience for Italian meta-physical thinker Giordano Bruno's lectures at Oxford University in the late 1500s. What does this have to do with the twentieth-century American experimental composer Robert Ashley and his opera for tele-vision, *Perfect Lives*? Nothing. Or everything, particularly if you take seriously Melody Sumner's question from her "Preface" to the libretto of the opera, when she asks if *Perfect Lives* is "actually a letter written to erstwhile friend, G. Bruno, back in the sixteenth century." While her question is rhetorical, and the answer is almost certainly no—although you can never be absolutely sure of anything with Ashley's work—it does bring to mind the last two lines of the libretto: "Dear George, what's going on? I'm not the same person that I used to be." Furthermore, the libretto *does* mention Bruno by name three times, and Ashley *did* say he was reading Frances Yates's work on Bruno while writing *Perfect Lives*. Bruno, incidentally, was burned alive in Rome in 1600 for heresy. So at the very least, Sumner's question makes an important point worth remembering. In all of Robert Ashley's music— most of which is operatic and theatrical in nature—everything means

Robert Ashley. © *Jack Mitchell, 1898. Used by permission*

something; everything is related; and everything makes reference to something else. Just when we think we know what's going on, the plot thickens. And where this whole chain of events gets started is Ashley's video opera, *Perfect Lives*, a work in seven thirty-minute episodes, set in early summer, in a small town in Illinois.

The basic theme of *Perfect Lives* (plot is too strong a word, implying, as it does, linearity without loose ends), concerns a middle-aged entertainer, Raoul de Noget, and his younger pal, Buddy, the World's Greatest Piano Player. The two travel the midwest circuit. One day, they find themselves in a small unnamed Illinois town, playing at the Perfect Lives Lounge. The two newcomers become friends with a couple of locals, the son and daughter of the Sheriff, and the four of them, as Ashley describes it, "hatch a plan to do something that, if they are caught doing it, it will be a crime, but if they are not caught it will be Art." The grand plan is to take all the money out of the local bank for one day, and then put it all back, something Ashley calls "a challenge . . . outside the realm of crime."

Fortunately, the Sheriff's son is also the assistant to the manager of the bank, and he is in a position to make sure that the bizarre scheme can actually work. The four conspirators soon learn that Gwyn, a teller in the bank, is planning to elope with Ed, and they decide to steal the money that day and put it in the elopement car. But when the Bank Manager discovers that the money is missing, the five remaining tellers—Jennifer, Kate, Eleanor, Linda, and Susie—perhaps because of the symbolic meaning of the moment, each has a religious experience that changes her life. At least, that's what we're led to believe. Meanwhile, the Sheriff and his wife, sitting in front of their fireplace at home, solve the mystery of the missing money, through what Ashley calls "a kind of catechism"; and Gwyn and Ed finally find a Justice of the Peace, although the marriage ceremony turns out to be what Ashley calls, "a ritual of medieval dimensions." The opera ends with a portrait of Isolde (the Sheriff's daughter and coconspirator in the bank caper) watching a picnic in the backyard, from the darkness of a doorway in her mother's house.

This short synopsis, of course, doesn't even begin to tell the whole story, much less do justice to the verbal subtleties, "in jokes," and subplots of the opera. Ashley is a master storyteller, and in his hands, this theme (or plot) becomes merely the formal construct for what is, in reality, his musings on life, told through the voices of everyday people. Ashley once said that he began to write *Perfect Lives* by talking to himself, every day, for as long as he could "focus on the image." As he told it, he had been interested in involuntary speech for quite some time, and recently had started doing "improvisations of speaking" that he associated with various characters. He said that as he began to collect these narratives, he realized that they were mainly things people had said to him, or ideas he associated with particular people that he knew. Ultimately, his libretto developed from this collection of sayings into an accumulation of short stories, each a minute or two long. Ashley said that what he was trying to do was "reproduce the music of the way people talk." He also said that the result he was after was not so much poetry, as song; not a refinement of language, but a huge number of small details that would make up a story. To his mind, part of the originality of *Perfect Lives* is that it draws from an earlier form of opera, one involved with "the idea of storytelling in music."

Ashley on Composing

Every musician I respect has a totally different system; there's nothing in common between them. My music is nothing like Terry Riley's music, or David Behrman's music, in the sense of having some common starting point.

The energy that keeps me working . . . is something that I've never been able to understand rationally. I've only had the experience of being able to see that energy objectively when the piece actually happens in front of me. When I hear it, then I say, "Yeah, I was right; or no, I was wrong."

I get obsessed with an idea, and it's almost an obligation. It totally dominates me. I have no control over it. It's not like a choice. . . . I get obsessed with a certain idea, and it takes over.

unpublished interview with the author, 1985

As a composer, Robert Ashley has always been interested in the theatrical aspects of music. Born in Ann Arbor, Michigan in 1930, he studied at the University of Michigan and then at the Manhattan School of Music in New York, thinking for a time that he would become a concert pianist. But he eventually came to the conclusion that he was merely imitating an exotic tradition—nineteenth-century European—that had little or nothing to do with his own everyday reality. So in the same way that he had given up jazz years earlier, he abandoned European music in favor of making his own. Back in Michigan by the late 1950s, Ashley became one of the founders of the legendary ONCE Festival (1960–67), thought to be the best of the many avant-garde festivals taking place during the sixties, and toured with the Sonic Arts Union for a decade, beginning in 1966. In 1969, he moved to California, becoming the director of the Center for

Contemporary Music at Mills College. In 1981, he left Mills and moved to New York.

Perfect Lives, which was written in New York, did not start out as a seven-part opera for television. In fact, the earliest version wasn't even called *Perfect Lives*, nor was the second. Ashley said that while he was talking to himself—creating all of these short songs—the possibility arose to record some of them for Lovely Music, an opportunity he described as a "catalyst event." This was in 1977, when Ashley was staying in New York, but still commuting to California a few months each year to his job at Mills College, where he lived in a hotel. He said that on this particular trip, he took "piles of paper" with him that were the beginnings of various portraits. There, in the recording studio at Mills, he began to combine these short songs into longer strings of songs, creating, over several days, two complete portraits or characterizations: Raoul and Isolde. These longer strings of songs he then spoke (sang) into a tape recorder in the Mills studio, in much the same way that he had been saying them to himself in New York. When the taping of his part was completed, he then asked a tabla player at the school to add a second part in imitation of his reading style. To this, Ashley and composer/pianist "Blue" Gene Tyranny, another colleague at Mills at the time, then added a series of chord sequences, which Tyranny played as background on the Polymoog. And over this, Tyranny then improvised in a style Ashley called "a special kind of piano playing—what everybody calls 'cocktail style.' [But] it's not. . . ." When it appeared, the album was called *Private Parts*, and Ashley said that the title was a musical joke based on the idea that everyone involved in the recording had operated independently of one another.

This early recorded version of *Private Parts* consisted of two episodes, "The Park" and "The Backyard." Eventually, these became the first and last sections of the opera *Perfect Lives*. Ashley then wrote "The Supermarket," "The Bank," "The Bar," "The Living Room," and "The Church," more or less in order. He said that by the time he finished the third episode, the project had, in his mind, become the seven-part opera it is today. This transformation from short songs to opera was helped along by The Kitchen, a downtown performance space in New York, which, in 1978, commissioned Ashley to create a work for television. He said that in trying to decide how to transform the material that he had already developed into a piece he could present on television, he got the idea of working in "templates."

Ashley on the Once Festival

God, we had huge audiences. I'm not bragging or anything, but the audiences were enormous.

unpublished interview with the author, 1985

A template, for Ashley, is the term he uses to describe "the subjective assignment of emotional values and moods to visual forms and corresponding musical structures." What this means is that because each episode of the opera is made up of a number of shorter songs, these short songs become the basic unit governing all of the other aspects of the piece, including the character of the playing, the orchestration, and the video imagery. In this sense, a template is a "profile," or "pattern" for reproducing a variety of parts, all with a similar form. The template of durations, for example, bases everything on seventy-two beats per minute, a number chosen because, with simple calculations, it can be used to control the relationship between film, video, music, and words. Ashley said, "It's like paint-by-numbers." He continued, "There's an overall metrical template for each of the seven songs . . . [that] governs the rate of speech and the inflection quality" for what becomes the music for the narrator. According to Ashley, "Within the rules defined by the templates, the collaborators . . . are free to interpret, 'improvise,' invent, and superimpose characteristics of their own artistic styles onto the texture of the work." In other words, the collaborators become "characters" in Ashley's opera, in essence creating their own personalities from Ashley's musical blueprints, much in the same way that performers in Duke Ellington's jazz band were, themselves, "a collection of characters." Ashley said he has always regarded swing bands "as proto-operas, and very American in form." He also suggested that *Perfect Lives* "is a kind of jazz narrative" that comes out of that tradition.

Ashley on his Background

I grew up outside of Ann Arbor, in the country, more or less out of touch with everybody. I learned that I wanted to be a musician from listening to records and from listening to the radio.

unpublished interview with the author, 1985

Another unifying factor Ashley used in composing *Perfect Lives* was the Evans-Wentz edition of *The Tibetan Book of the Dead*, in particular, the essays about how the text was used traditionally. In Tibetan culture, there is a belief that when someone dies, the senses disappear at different rates, with the sense of hearing being the last to go. The traditional use of the book is that, at death, the text is shouted into the person's ear, providing instruction for the coming experience of death and reincarnation forty-nine days later. Ashley said he became amused by the idea that talking into a microphone, and guiding an audience through the intricacies of his music, was essentially the same basic idea. He also said that while he didn't use the philosophical ideas of the book in the opera, he did begin to think of *Perfect Lives* as similar in form to *The Tibetan Book of the Dead*, complete with seven chambers, and characters representing good and evil. Perhaps this is why Ashley once described *Perfect Lives* as a "comic opera about reincarnation."

Although *Perfect Lives* was designed for television, it was performed in various concert and stage versions first. Between 1978 and 1983, versions of the opera were presented in the United States and Europe some twenty-seven times, including, in 1982, a weeklong run in London's Almeida Theatre, where filmmaker Peter Greenaway made a documentary film about Ashley and the opera for British television. Ashley's own film of *Perfect Lives* received its broadcast premiere on Channel Four Television in Great Britain in April 1984 in the "late night" spot, meaning that it was on at 10:30 every night for a week. The response was such that it was replayed the following year.

If the narrative structure of Ashley's *Perfect Lives* sounds a bit involved and convoluted, consider for a moment the direction his work took from there. *Perfect Lives* became the middle of a trilogy of operas that, according to Ashley, trace the history of consciousness as it moves across America from east to west. The first opera, *Atalanta* (Acts of God), written after *Perfect Lives* and premiered in 1986, focuses on the East Coast, and looks toward Europe. The second, *Perfect Lives*, takes place in Illinois. And the third, *Now Eleanor's Idea*, deals with the West Coast. This structure may sound reasonable enough until we realize that *Now Eleanor's Idea* is actually subdivided into four additional operas: *Improvement (Don Leaves Linda)*, *Foreign Experiences*, *Now Eleanor's Idea* (the "title song" of the quartet), and *The Immortality Songs*. And as if this weren't enough, this last work, *The Immortality Songs*, itself splits into forty-nine independent operas, the first of which is *eL/Aficionado*, premiered in New York in 1991. And if you can keep all this straight, then reflect back to the fact that Eleanor was one of the five bank tellers from the first opera, *Perfect Lives*, who saw something that changed her life.

Ashley on the Wolfman

I could never get it loud enough. . . . It's actually designed to go *beyond* loud. In those days [1960s], the speakers were so small that it only sounded loud . . . . It's supposed to go beyond loud, where you don't even think that it's loud anymore.

unpublished interview with the author, 1985

Given such a complicated narrative structure—stretching as it does from Greek mythology to *Low Rider* magazine—is it any wonder that Ashley's work is frequently misunderstood? Perhaps too much attention has been given to the role of improvisation and collaboration in his music, and not enough to the correlation of structure and detail, and the Neoplatonic (Atomist) concept of the universe mirrored in the structure of its smallest detail. For Ashley, "That's Giordano Bruno. If this is the model of the world, you have to live with it." Critic and composer Kyle Gann, writing in *The Village Voice* in 1991, suggested that when the twenty-first century looks back to see how the future of opera developed, Robert Ashley, like Monteverdi of the sixteenth century, will look like a radical new beginning. As Gann sees it, "It remains an underground secret that Ashley is the only *original* opera composer of the late 20th century, the first since Harry Partch to tell the European tradition to go to hell."

ᔐ 18 ᔐ

O Superman

LAURIE ANDERSON

1983

Good evening. This is your Captain.

Laurie Anderson has a knack for knowing just what to say, and exactly when to say it. Her lines are famous. She's a performance artist, and talking is what she does best, though that's not all she does. Onstage, she combines her tales about life at the end of the century with films, slides, and videos, all backed by an art-rock band in which she plays some of the most up-to-date, high-tech gizmos around, with people like David Van Tieghem and Adrian Belew. The result is a stage show, at once sophisticated, but vulnerable; entertaining, but definitely on the edge. Anderson said she had no idea her work had any real crowd appeal until she was booked by accident into a country & western bar in Houston, where her "show" was accepted equally by both the art crowd in the audience as well as the regular patrons of the bar, who saw her as a person who just told some stories and played the violin. As Anderson said, "They got it perfectly."

Let X=X.

Laurie Anderson. *Lynn Goldsmith/© Corbis*

The key to understanding Laurie Anderson's new type of artistry—and, by implication, the whole genre of performance art—is to remember that Anderson has *always* maintained an interest in doing several things at once, although she has *never* identified any one of them as defining what it is that she does. And since she has never defined herself in anything close to traditional terms, the public doesn't seem able to label her either. So some quarter-century after the term was first coined, most of us still don't know what it is that performance artists do. But we know we like them. We know it's a new genre; it's not just a fad. And we know that Laurie Anderson is the most famous performance artist in the world, the first to hit the big time, a superstar—record contract, movie deal, and a cult following, plus a state-of-the-art home studio always on call.

You know, I've got this funny feeling I've seen this all before.

Along the way, or course, there have been numerous attempts to define performance art. One such moment occurred in February 1983, when Anderson's magnum opus, *United States*—a four-part, eight-hour, two-evening event in seventy-eight sections—was presented in its entirety at the Brooklyn Academy of Music. At the time, *Newsweek* called the still relatively new medium of performance art a "catchall genre," categorizing it as "the theatricalization of just about anything." *Time*, on the other hand, saw it as an "avant-garde hybrid" with roots in Dada and the Happenings of the '60s. While critic John Rockwell, in his book *All American Music*, published in 1983, compared Anderson's work to that of art-rock star Patti Smith, saying both had begun as admired cult poets, and both had then sung their words to "proto-minimalist rock." Rockwell also saw a connection between Anderson's stage show and the "post-Cageian avant-garde theater of composers like [Robert] Ashley," and said he thought her work was "best described as solo opera." Anderson describes herself as a storyteller, and says that "all the other stuff—the politics and the music and the pictures—are really just ways of expanding on the story and learning to tell it in different ways." She says she has always "tried not to make any distinction between visual things and aural things," adding, "They come totally from the same sensibility."

Anderson on Her Work

If I had to define my work, it would probably have something to do with time: how I try to stretch it, compress it, turn it into a couple of ice cubes, spread it all over the place, or turn it into air.

Talking Music, 1995

Traditional plays invent characters and predict their postplay lives. My approach leaves me freer to be disjunctive and jagged, and to focus on incidents, ideas, collisions. Personally I feel closer to the attitude of the stand-up comedian—not only because I believe that laughter is powerful, but because the comedian works in real time.

Musician, April 1984

This is the time. And this is the record of the time.

Laurie Anderson said there was a time, just before high school, when she practiced six hours a day, and "had some fantasies" about playing violin professionally. The problem was, she felt equally divided between music and art. For her, a typical Saturday during her childhood (she was born in 1947), was spent in Chicago, some fifty miles from her home in Wayne, playing in the Chicago Youth Symphony in the morning, and going to painting classes at the Art Institute in the afternoon, a day she later described as "always split right down the middle." But when she was sixteen, she suddenly quit playing the violin. She said she came to the realization that a professional musician, much like a professional athlete, is limited to only one instrument, one sport, one activity. As she put it, "I thought that I would either play the violin all the time or not play it at all. I chose not to play." Proud of this decision today, Anderson says that, back then, she loved books and painting too much to give them up; and besides, there were too many other things she wanted to learn.

Anderson on Her Childhood

My mother played the violin. All the kids were more or less forced to play an instrument . . . because my parents thought it would be nice to have an orchestra.

Talking Music, 1995

We had a big record collection. I would listen to the same record for a few days and then go on to another one. I liked the spoken records more than the music.

Talking Music, 1995

Big Science. Hallelujah. Big Science. Yodellayheehoo.

After high school, Anderson, describing herself as an excellent student for all the wrong reasons, went to Mills College in Oakland, California to major in biology. Once there, however, she decided that she had chosen the wrong field, saying she soon realized she liked drawing the graphs "more for the color" than for the biological information they contained. So after a year at Mills, she transferred to Barnard College (Columbia University) in New York to major in art history. Anderson said that during her college years, she didn't have anything to do with music, didn't own a record collection, and didn't go to concerts. What she liked were the talk shows on the radio. In 1970, for an exhibition of sound sculptures at New York's School of Visual Design, she created "voices that were up in boxes on very tall stilts." She said the idea of her stories coming out of boxes had come to her from listening to the radio. After Barnard (which she left magna cum laude and Phi Beta Kappa), Anderson studied for a year at the School of Visual Arts with Sol LeWitt and Carl Andre, drawn there by a strong sculpture department and the excitement of being at the center of "minimal art and minimal art theory." But she stayed only one year, returning to Columbia to study sculpture. And although she was thrown out four times—her work wasn't always considered weighty enough by the Columbia faculty—she completed an MFA there in 1972.

Hi. I'm not home right now.

In 1973, music began to reemerge in Anderson's work. The piece *Automotive* was a concert for cars, "nice cars in harmony," as she described them to the New York radio station that broadcast a tape of the event. A year later, Anderson took up the violin again, although this time, seldom using it as an actual musical instrument. Instead, the violin became a prop. Once, she even filled it with water and tried to play it. Another time, she had herself frozen in ice skates into a block of ice, planning to play until she melted free. Along the way, Anderson has used many visual devices on stage, such as a neon bow à la *Star Wars*, and a glow-in-the-dark violin. But her most famous "prop" is the early "tape bow violin" from 1975. By replacing the violin strings with a tape playback head, and the hairs of the bow with a piece of magnetic recording tape on which a slogan was prerecorded, Anderson created the tape bow violin—a postmodern juxtaposition of image and effect, meaning, essentially, that the actions we see her make with the instrument are not in agreement with the sounds we hear. For example, moving the entire length of the bow across the tape head (a traditional gesture in violin playing, after all) allows the complete slogan, or any other short sentence for that matter, to "speak." Shorter bow-arm movements produce words, phrases, or, perhaps, stuttering. According to Anderson's notes from this period, the first slogan she chose was "Ethics Is the Esthetics of the Future." In performance, she reportedly built slowly from individual words to phrases to the complete slogan, before concluding with "Ethics Is the Esthetics of the Few, of the Few, of the Few . . . ture."

Well you don't know me, but I know you.

During the mid to late 1970s, Laurie Anderson was a denizen of the downtown New York art and music scene, sometimes writing criticism for art magazines. She also taught art history at a local college, a job that lasted until she made up one too many story/lectures about the slides, got caught, and was fired. But these were day jobs. Anderson saw herself as an artist, creating jukebox installations, and hanging out in lofts with other artists, listening to five-hour rehearsals by Philip Glass. The point at which Anderson's own individual pieces began to coalesce into something larger and more substantial came in 1979, the year she premiered *Americans on the Move* at Carnegie Recital Hall. The piece was commissioned by gallery owner Holly Solomon to celebrate her husband's birthday. Anderson said she began to think of *Americans on the Move* as part of a continuing series when she realized how much fun she was having working on it. She also said that was the moment when *Americans on the Move* became the first version of *United States.*

You can come as you are, but pay as you go.

As Anderson began actively planning the expanded *United States*, she conceived it as being in four sections that would be about transportation, politics, money, and love. The material from *Americans on the Move* went into Part 1. Then, unexpectedly, a song from Part 2, "O Superman (for Massenet)," took on a life of it's own. Released originally as a single, backed by "Walk the Dog," "O Superman," as everybody called it, became a hit on the British rock singles charts, rising to No. 2 in 1981, and selling nearly 800,000 copies worldwide by 1983. Although it didn't scale similar heights in America, where the charts are more conservative, it did yield a record deal with Warner Bros., tour support, and a CD, *Big Science*, Anderson's first commercial album, released in 1982.

Anderson on Opera and Singing

In opera, the words are not the most important things. . . . They're an excuse for the opera singers to use their voices beautifully. My work is just the opposite. If the words are somewhat sung, it's almost like extended talking, pitched talking. It's certainly not *bel canto*. I'm much more interested in speaking rhythms and in words themselves than in singing.

Musician, April 1984

Hello? This is your mother. Are you there?

"O Superman," the song that first brought Laurie Anderson to public attention, was one of the earlier songs written for *United States*. As such, it has elements of both high-tech wizardry and early do-it-yourself installation days. Dark and political, "O Superman" is a typical Anderson story, full of funny lines and thought-provoking clichés; laced with an attitude, simultaneously accepting, sympathetic, and critical; told and sung over a looped rhythmic vocal accompaniment ("ha ha ha ha"); and overlapped with parts spoken or sung in harmony with herself, thanks to the Vocoder (a then state-of-the-art instrument), capable of splitting and transforming the sound of Anderson's words into an eerie chorus of voices. At almost eight and a half minutes long, "O Superman" was an unlikely candidate for the pop charts, even in England. But Anderson's words are compelling. And Superman is, after all, a twentieth-century archetype; we all know something about him. And the atmosphere Anderson creates, even on a recording, is strong, thought-provoking, and real. "Here come the planes," delivered in a somewhat sinister manner through a Vocoder chorus of voices, still had apocalyptic implications in 1981. "They're American planes. Made in

America. Smoking or non-smoking?" didn't comfort us all that much either. Nor, come to think of it, did "O Mom and Dad, Mom and Dad."

Oh boy. Right again.

The premiere of *United States*, Parts 1–4, was a much anticipated event in downtown New York in February 1983. Individual pieces from the first two sections had already been heard other places and even recorded. And both sections had been previously performed, Part 1 at the Kitchen, Part 2 at the Orpheum Theater (a bigger space), sponsored by the Kitchen. But Parts 3 and 4 were new, with Part 4 a commission from the Brooklyn Academy of Music. Onstage, Anderson was the center of attention, with her spiked punk hair, red socks, black clothes. She reminded Jack Kroll of *Newsweek* of "other lithe, black-clad prowlers like the young Lenny Bruce and the young Mort Sahl." He also said she made him think of a "cybernetic Lily Tomlin." Calling *United States* "a dense weaving of odd, smart anecdotes and stories," *New York* magazine said Anderson explored "the bewildering cuckoo quality of life in high-tech society." And *Time* called the endeavor "part narrative epic, part rock opera, part home movie." Rockwell, writing for the *New York Times*, said Anderson had "forged a new kind of musical theater, helped create a whole new audience, and pointed a way for the opera of the future."

Language is a virus from outer space.

In 1984, Anderson, now a celebrity recognized in restaurants, told *Musician* magazine that if she had a message to give the world, she wouldn't make slides and films, and write songs. They were all too inefficient for that. She said she would write her message down on a piece of paper, as clearly as she could, and hand it out to everyone. For her, this distinction between ways and means was "the whole difference between art and ideas." As she quipped, "Art is a sensual experience, I never check the facts." She also said she thought most things were sufficiently weird, that just describing them was strange

enough. To Anderson's way of thinking, "You don't have to be a surreal-
ist to think the world is strange."

It's a sky-blue sky. Satellites are out tonight.

Ten years after the initial success of "O Superman" and *United States*—a
decade of tours, a movie *(Home of the Brave)*, numerous CDs, appear-
ances on late-night talk shows, and the hosting of a PBS series with her
computer-created clone—Laurie Anderson says there are problems with
success. "Sometimes it makes it harder to work," she admits, adding that
"you can get so sure of what is expected of you that you actually start to
do that." But "that's very stupid," according to her. Saying she has always
tried to do the unexpected, Anderson concludes, "But it is hard sometimes to be simple."

She said: It goes. That's the way it goes. It goes that way.

19

Miserere

ARVO PÄRT

1989

It starts so quietly and with such hesitation, we're not sure it has even begun. We hear one voice, male, slowly singing words and syllables of words, surrounded by silence, intoning the *Miserere*, on a sacred text that Estonian composer Arvo Pärt took from the Vulgate Bible, Psalm 50: *Miserere mei, Deus*; Have mercy upon me, O God. Composed in 1989, the *Miserere* is written in what Pärt calls his "tintinnabuli" style, a word that loosely translates from the Latin (his chosen language for vocal music) as the sounds of bells. Pärt first began writing in this style some thirteen years earlier, in 1976. Seven new pieces were completed that year. Before that, he had written almost nothing since 1968, just two transitional pieces, a cantata and a symphony. It was a turning point in his life, and marked the end of a creative silence of over seven years.

As the *Miserere* continues a clarinet enters, trailing the voice with the outlines of chords unfolding as isolated points of sound; later, a bass clarinet plays a drone. Slowly, other instruments appear, hover near the voice, and move on. Some hear a relationship to minimalism in this music. But while Pärt does use repetitive processes and structures, his minimalism is not fast and rhythmic like that of Reich and Glass, but patterned, introspective, and often slow. Few people hear traditional

Arvi Pärt. *Photo by Robert Masotti. Used by permission*

minimalist manipulation as this music's primary goal. Eventually, a second voice enters, joining the first, both voices entwining, becoming one. Pärt calls this process the "kernel" of his style, and says it is expressible by the equation: $1 + 1 = 1$.

Understanding how two voices can become one is essential to understanding Pärt's tintinnabuli style. According to Paul Hillier, whose *Arvo Pärt* (1997) is the only book-length study available on the composer, the basis of the tintinnabuli style "is a two-part texture (working always note against note), consisting of a 'melodic' voice moving mostly by step . . . and a 'tintinnabuli' voice sounding the notes of the tonic triad." In his analyses of Pärt's music, Hillier continually refers to the M-voice and T-voice as two aspects of one interwoven melody. He says that Pärt told him the M-voice "always signifies the subjective world, the daily egoistic life of sin and suffering," while the T-voice represents "the objective realm of forgiveness." Hillier likened Pärt's description to "the eternal dualism of body and spirit, earth and heaven," and said it would be foolish for anyone to attempt to understand Pärt's music without taking into account his "particular mode of spiritual thought" (primarily Russian Orthodoxy), and his growing sense of spirituality. It is worth remembering that although the majority of Pärt's music from 1976 on is intended for the concert hall, it is almost all entirely spiritual in nature.

The *Miserere* is somewhat unusual in Pärt's body of work, because it is the result of combining two different pieces, written years apart. As the third verse of Psalm 50 ends, by now with all five soloists singing and the timpani moving "from background to foreground in a massive crescendo," to use Hillier's words, the *Miserere* psalm is suddenly replaced by the full chorus and a wall-of-sound *Dies irae*, Day of wrath. This music is not new, however, but is a reworking of Pärt's thirteen-year-old work *Calix*. Pärt's version of this ancient chant—a text and melody associated with the dead for over a thousand years—is based, not on the more well-known *Dies irae* melody from Gregorian chant, but on the equally powerful, though lesser-known *Dies irae* from the Russian Orthodox rite. The borrowing from ancient sources continues, producing a setting of the music as a three-part mensuration canon, a time-scaling procedure used in the fifteenth and sixteenth centuries.

Pärt's twentieth-century result, to quote Hillier again, is "a series of descending A minor scales (with attendant T-voices) heard simultaneously in five tempi, each one progressively doubling the length of the notes so that the slowest is 16 times longer than the fastest."

After seven stanzas of the *Dies irae*, the slower, more pensive and introspective *Miserere* psalm returns, this new beginning once more signaled by a solo voice: *Tibi soli peccavi*; Against thee only have I sinned. Pärt sets these sixteen remaining verses of Psalm 50 for the five soloists, omitting the chorus, and separating the verses by four instrumental interludes. The sound of bells, a continuing influence on Pärt since the 1970s, comes in. At the end, the chorus returns with the eighth verse of the *Dies irae*: *Rex tremendae majestatis*; King of awful majesty. But unlike its previous manifestation, this final music is transformed, the mood and focus altered from abject suffering to one of hope. For Hillier, this final verse is "no longer anguished, . . . but hushed in awe."

For most listeners living in the West in the early 1980s, the music of Arvo Pärt seemed to come, fully formed and in great abundance, from out of nowhere. For the most part, this delay in recognition was caused by the Cold War between the Soviet Union and the West. Pärt had been active as a composer since the early 1960s, but most of his performances had occurred behind the Iron Curtain, in places like Moscow, Leningrad, Zagreb, and Tallinn, the capital of Estonia. Estonian by birth, Pärt was born in a small town some fifty miles southeast of Tallinn, in 1935. As a child, he attended an after-school music school, and practiced on a beat-up Russian grand piano his mother had managed to acquire. Hillier said only the outer octaves still worked properly, and suggested this gave Pärt his first encouragement to experiment with writing music of his own. As a student, Pärt not only played the piano, but also sang in the chorus. In the orchestra, he played oboe; and in the dance band, he played drums. When drafted for compulsory service in 1954, he was able to spend both years playing oboe and snare drum in a military orchestra. After the service, he entered the Tallinn Conservatory, studying composition with Heino Eller, himself a former student of the Russian composer Alexander Glazunov. Eller's own music was conservative, but he allowed his students freedom to explore the new ideas from the West.

One fortunate result of the official cultural thaw of 1957–58 was that Arnold Schoenberg's music was no longer banned in the Soviet Union. With this newfound freedom, Pärt began studying the few 12-tone scores available to him in Estonia, and working through the only two books of 12-tone exercises he could find, books by Ernst Krenek and Herbert Eimert.

While still a student at the conservatory, Arvo Pärt became the first Estonian composer to write music using Schoenberg's 12-tone technique. The piece was *Nekrolog*, an orchestral work finished in 1960. The title means obituary. Although only parts of *Nekrolog* make use of the serial technique, it was enough to attract the attention of the Third All-Union Congress of Composers in Moscow in 1962. There, Pärt came under sharp criticism from First Secretary Khrennikov, who said of *Nekrolog*, "We see that the attempts to employ the expressive techniques of the avant-garde bourgeois music for the realization of progressive ideas of our time are discredited by the results they produce." Pärt's explanation was that "nothing was considered more hostile than so-called influences from the West, to which 12-tone music belonged."

Pärt on His Tintinnabuli Style

Tintinnabulation is an area I sometimes wander into when I am searching for answers—in my life, my music, my work.

notes to **Tabula Rasa***, ECM*

I have discovered that it is enough when a single note is beautifully played. This one note, or a silent beat, or a moment of silence, comforts me. I work with very few elements—with one voice, with two voices. I build with the most primitive materials—with the triad, with one specific tonality. The three notes of the triad are like bells. And this is why I called it tintinnabulation.

notes to **Tabula Rasa***, ECM*

I could compare my music to white light which contains all colours. Only a prism can divide the colours and make them appear; this prism could be the spirit of the listener.

ECM brochure, 1991

Throughout much of the 1960s, Arvo Pärt continued to compose in a 12-tone style, employing with it a collage technique that Hillier said might, on the surface, remind us of Berg and Bartók, or, perhaps, Penderecki and Ligeti. The deeper influences, he identified as "the great composers of the European tradition," with an emphasis on Tchaikovsky and Glazunov. Pärt's own music, however, was anything but traditional. His next problem with Soviet authorities came in 1968, over his work *Credo*, for piano, chorus, and orchestra. Still written in a 12-tone/collage style in which tonal sections are juxtaposed against atonal ones, the *Credo* encountered trouble from the beginning, primarily because of its title and the religious nature of its words—I believe in Jesus Christ—which the Soviet authorities judged to be gestures of defiance. The music itself, however, was actually based on Bach's Prelude in C Major from Book One of the *Well-Tempered Clavier*. In the words of critic K. Robert Schwarz, "Pärt progressively fragments and distorts the Bach until it achieves a screaming, hellish climax—and then he allows the simple purity of the Prelude to re-emerge triumphantly." Nevertheless, performances of *Credo* were banned in the Soviet Union for the next ten years. And Pärt, the composer, for this and other reasons more personal, fell silent.

Arvo Pärt's seven-year silence as a composer was not, in reality, a total silence. While the cantata written during this period contains little of interest today, the Third Symphony from 1971 is definitely a transitional work, showing the growing influence of early music on Pärt's style. Apparently, this "silent" time offered him the chance to completely reconsider and redesign his way of writing music. As he described it to Hillier later, he used the time to "learn how to walk again as a composer." Driven by an instinctive knowledge that early music held answers for him, Pärt had already begun to study Gregorian chant. From there, he moved through thirteenth-century polyphonic writing to Renaissance masses and motets, studying the music of composers like Johannes Ockeghem and Josquin Desprez. Hillier says that during this period Pärt would sometimes try writing "semi-automatically," experimenting with drawing shapes, and trying to fill them with melody; or try quickly reading a text, and "write music to mirror." He calls this

Pärt's "purification" of his musical roots, and says that about this same time, Pärt also "became highly sensitized to all noise, and separated himself from all other musical life," including, for a time, performances of his own music.

Slowly, Pärt's new "tintinnabuli" style developed, a combination of his growing spirituality, plus his continued interest in early music, minimalism, and bells. Tonality reemerged. The triad, the scale, and the arpeggio once again became important. And as the idea of two voices becoming one became accepted, and the practice of relying on the basic elements of triad and diatonic scale to produce music became common practice, the essential characteristics of tintinnabuli music emerged. Basically, the tintinnabuli style is Pärt's system for relating melody and harmony; a way of reconciling the horizontal and vertical aspects of pitch. His solution was to create two voices that exist in a fixed relationship to each other. One voice, related to scales, moves mostly by step. The other voice, existing primarily as arpeggiated triads, fills in notes from the tonic chord. The two voices intertwine within a strict set of rules. In Pärt's mind, they become one. The music this system produces is diatonic, without any chromaticism, or even a change of key. Harmony does not function here in the traditional way; there are no chord progressions providing tension and release. Instead, Pärt's sounds seem to hover in air, suspended, causing Hillier to suggest that what we hear is better described as "a single moment spread out in time." He also said Pärt's new style developed intuitively, and that the term tintinnabuli was added at the end.

Arvo Pärt's creative silence ended in 1976, when his new style was unveiled in a three-year period of unabated compositional activity. During this time many of his most well-known pieces were written, including *Fratres* and *Tabula Rasa*, as well as an early version of the *Passio*. The first compositions of this new approach, *Modus* and *Calix*, while not yet completely in the tintinnabuli style, deserve consideration for a moment. The title of *Modus*, like other of Pärt's titles from Soviet days, is a camouflage, designed to slip music with a religious theme past the censors and onto the stage. Once this became unnecessary, Pärt restored the real title, *Sarah Was Ninety Years Old*. And *Calix*, whose title means chalice or cup, is Pärt's 1976 setting of the *Dies irae*, the one he modified thirteen years later to use in the *Miserere*.

Pärt on Composing

A composition comes as a single gesture which is already, in essence, music. The path to this is hard; you descend to the lowest spiritual plane, the bottom of the world, not knowing what will be found. The only thing you know is that you don't know anything. If this gesture, like a seed, takes root, it must be cultivated with extreme care so that it may grow; meanwhile you are oscillating between heaven and earth. The compositional task is to find the appropriate system for the gesture. It is one's capacity for suffering that gives the energy to create.

University of Oregon, 1994, from Paul Hillier, **Arvo Pärt**

Perhaps if Arvo Pärt had elected to stay in Estonia, he would have remained relatively unknown to listeners in the West. Neither he nor his second wife, Nora, wished to leave. Plus, Pärt had, from student days, lived in relative comfort, thanks, first, to steady work as a recording engineer with Estonian Radio, and, later, the chance to compose for theater and film. (It is estimated that Pärt wrote some fifty film scores, although he considers them of no importance today.) The family's circumstances changed in the 1970s, however. The combination of a hardening of the official attitude toward his music, plus the subsequent refusal to allow him to travel abroad, made his life difficult. That, coupled with the fact that his wife was Jewish and the officially sanctioned exodus of Soviet Jews to Israel during the 1970s offered an opportunity some were encouraging him to take, finally convinced Pärt and his family to move. Leaving Estonia in 1980, Pärt, his wife, and two sons traveled by train on a two-day trip to Vienna. There, they were met unexpectedly by a representative of the publishing house Universal Edition, who offered them help and a chance to stay in Vienna. In 1981, they moved to Berlin.

Once Arvo Pärt emigrated to the West, his popularity quickly increased, due, in large part, to the German recording giant ECM, which began issuing recordings of his music, much of it performed by the

Hilliard Ensemble, at that time still led by Paul Hillier. The first release was *Tabula Rasa* in 1984. The *Miserere* was released in 1991. The premiere of an early version of the *Miserere* had taken place in Rouen in 1986. While some critics of Pärt's music were quick to label it "holy minimalism," the majority of listeners, most of whom viewed Pärt more as a musical mystic, found his music calming, uplifting, and serene, a welcome oasis of sound in a century where atonal complexity appeared to reign. And minimalist or not, Pärt's music did play a leading role in the emerging phenomenon of "spiritual minimalism" (to use Schwarz's term), a movement of the late 1980s and early 1990s that saw the emergence of Henryk Gorecki from Poland and England's John Tavener (two composers often linked with Pärt), as well as the a worldwide resurgence of interest in chant. Arvo Pärt, however, remained unfazed by success. Himself a bit of a recluse, seldom even giving interviews, his music of the past quarter-century exists like an icon, sounding proof of the sacred power of music. For Pärt, his music is a form of worship. And to his mind, "Art has to deal with eternal questions, not just sorting out the issues of today."

20

Atlas

MEREDITH MONK

1991

Meredith Monk was a performance artist long before they invented the term. In fact, she's one of the reasons they invented it. For most of her life, she has thought of her voice and her body as forming two parts "of a single expressive instrument," an instrument that reveals itself in staged and filmed rituals and "operas" of movement, color, and sound. The center of it all is Monk's universe of voices, voices that "sing and dance . . . moan and yodel . . . squeal, gurgle and whisper," to borrow the words of K. Robert Schwarz.

Although Monk has always considered herself a composer, her critics have never been exactly sure what her category is. Even her own press material lists composer, singer, filmmaker, director, and choreographer. Others have labeled Monk a mime. The *New York Times* added "story-teller, historian and prophet" to the list in 1996, then went on to say that she can even resemble an "explorer" or an "archeologist" at times. Monk herself said the confusion—although it was never that to her—all began one day in 1965. She was sitting at the piano practicing, when, she says, she "had a revelation." What she realized was that she could go beyond the mere development of her own "style of singing." The way she saw it, she had the potential to choreograph her voice, much in the same way as she

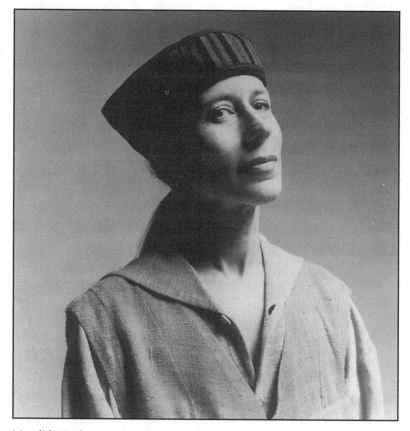

Meredith Monk. *Photo by Michael O'Neill. Used by permission*

did her body. Suddenly, she said, a new musical world opened up before her, her voice populated by "all these characters and landscapes within it." "In a flash," she said, "I saw where I would go from that point on."

Monk on Her Voice

In each song, I'm looking for *the* voice, you know. And I'm very much interested that each song have a very particular kind of character. I don't mean "character" in a literal sense necessarily, but that it, in a way, creates a world in itself. So I'm always trying to find new ones. I don't want to hear a voice that I've done before.

Talking Music, 1995

I have about three [octaves]. On a good day, I have about E♭ below middle C to E♭ above high C. I can scream higher, but that's about my working range.

Talking Music, 1995

Where Monk had been, prior to this revelation, was Sarah Lawrence College, a school just north of New York City. She had graduated from there the year before. But as for where Monk was born, that answer depended on which reference book you happened to read. Several say she was born in Lima, Peru, in 1942, but that's only because she once grew tired of having to give the same answers in interview after interview. She says she regrets it now, the biographical confusion and all. The truth is, Monk really comes from New York, the city and the suburbs. Her mother, whose Russian side of the family included an operatic bass, a concert pianist, and a cantor, sang popular songs and advertising jingles on the radio—Royal pudding, Duz soap, Muriel cigars—at a time when broadcasting was still done live. Monk said that by the time she was three, she was not only traveling with her mother to jobs and auditions, she was also enrolled in both piano lessons and Dalcroze Eurythmics, an educational system for children combining music, movement, and improvisation that, she says, "teaches music through the body." That's how Monk thinks she learned it. As she says, "I never seem to separate sound and music and space—they seem to all be one to me."

By the time Monk graduated from Sarah Lawrence College in 1964—with a degree that had allowed her to create a cross-disciplinary program of study around music, theater, film, and dance—she considered herself an experienced performer, although, she confesses now, one with that twenty-one-year-old arrogant sense of self. In her case, however, this confidence was not misplaced. Within a year of returning to the city, Monk wrote *16 Millimeter Earrings,* her 1966 autobiographical multimedia collage, an ambitious work of dance, music, films, and props that took her away from the more traditional worlds of music and dance and into performance art. Monk saw it as her breakthrough work; listeners heard it as the arrival of a unique new voice in the arts.

Monk on Her Early Influences

I remember hearing *The Rite of Spring* when I was about twelve . . . and
I remember just being so blown away and so moved by it. I just couldn't
believe it. It was amazing. . . . After I left college, the Beatles were really
important to me, because I felt that a lot of what they were doing was
very close to what we were doing in the arts. . . . It was an interesting
time for me to grow up, because while that was a rite of passage for me,
it was also, because rock and roll was coming in, a change of world.

Talking Music, 1995

I've always loved medieval music. I love music through Bach and then
go to the twentieth century. One of my absolute favorites is Perotinus.

*Edward Strickland, **American Composers**, 1991*

By the late 1960s, Meredith Monk was creating large-scale performance pieces that explored and extended the relationship between performer and audience. She did this by presenting her work as a series of
"installments," each event separated by long periods of time. *Juice*, for
example, her multimedia music-theater work from 1969, was performed
in a series of three "installments" taking place over six weeks. One ticket
gained admission to all events. The first event, and the largest, occurred
on the spiraling ramp inside the Guggenheim Museum. The audience
was seated on the floor below, looking up in all directions. Among other
things, the production included a chorus of eighty-five singer/dancers
playing Jew's harps, a rider on horseback in front of the museum, people
in period costumes, and four solo characters "painted red from head to
toe." The job of the red people was to journey slowly up the spiral ramp
of the museum as the various events took place. At one point, the entire
chorus ran by them. And although it all sounds suspiciously like a "happening," it wasn't. Everything was planned and exactly timed to focus
the attention of the audience from one part of the building to another.
Monk said she was thinking a lot about architecture at the time.

The next installment of *Juice* occurred five weeks later in a smaller
theater, the Minor Latham Playhouse, at Barnard College. Here, Monk

said her idea was to create "a kind of zoom lens in," where time and experience felt compressed. Fewer performers were involved in this second event, and the four red people, of whom Monk was one, became the focal point of the work. The horse and rider from the museum became, in this installment, a person on a hobby horse. And as other material from the Guggenheim event was reintroduced, it too was changed and rescaled in ways intended to play on the memory of the viewer. Monk said her interest lay in trying to combine a resonance from the past with the experience of the present. She wanted to see if the two could exist simultaneously.

The third, and final, installment of *Juice* took place one week later, in a small loft space capable of holding only a few people at a time. This event was an installation, without live performers. It consisted of a place in which to view a videotape of the faces of the four people in red, plus a display of the outfits and props from the Guggenheim event: eighty-five white costumes, eighty-five Jew's harps, eighty-five pairs of red combat boots. The horse in this installment became a tiny figurine placed in the room. Monk said another thing she was trying to do with *Juice* was stretch the idea of going to the theater, until it became an entirely different kind of ritual.

In the 1970s, Meredith Monk, while not entirely abandoning her other projects, embarked on a solo career. During this period, she purposefully extended her vocal technique into new areas, created new material for her voice, and toured extensively. John Rockwell, writing in the early 1980s, characterized Monk's singing as "original and inventive extensions of a wide range of third-world vocal techniques," but said they were "emitted over mostly lulling, simply triadic, repetitive instrumental accompaniment." While Rockwell thought that the harmonic basis of Monk's music was too simplistic, K. Robert Schwarz, writing later, felt that Monk complimented her singing with "burbling keyboard patterns, built up from the repetition and transformation of brief melodic cells." He added that while the accompaniment, if not the singing, owed a debt to minimalism, "these simple, repeated melodies possess a haunting beauty." Monk, on the other hand, has always maintained that she is *not* a minimalist. As she told Kyle Gann, "I come from a folk music tradition. I was a folksinger with a guitar. The repetition in my music I think of as being like folk music: you have your chorus and verse." In 1978, Monk, citing a desire to work with additional voices, founded Meredith Monk and Vocal Ensemble, a group she continues to tour and record with today. She has also continued her solo career.

Monk on Her Music

I like to think that I'm starting from scratch each time. In some way, that makes it very hard because I don't have anything that I can take for granted myself. So it's a mystery to me, when I start, what it's going to be.

Talking Music, 1995

I don't really know where some of this music comes from in me.

American Composers, 1991

I like the idea of making music that has a mythic quality or dimension. I don't think of a particular myth, but I like the way that myth itself is a way of translating the world that we live in into a different dimension that everybody can participate in.

Talking Music, 1995

When audiences come to our concerts, it often takes them a while to figure out that they can have a good time. But then they do. Art doesn't always have to be totally serious.

American Composers, 1991

Meredith Monk says that in most of her music, whether theater pieces or film, she tries "to express a sense of timelessness; of time as a circle or recurring cycle." *Book of Days*, her 1988 film, was, in her mind, "very much about the transparency and relativity of time." In this film, Monk weaves together strands of narrative, music, and images, to create a tapestry of fourteenth-century Europe, and of a young girl living there, disoriented by twentieth-century visions. These flashbacks and flash-forwards take place in the mind of Eva, who is portrayed by Monk. As the story travels back and forth between centuries—from the plague to AIDS, automobiles to Noah's ark—the past is depicted in black and white, the present is in color. Monk says that it's this sense of displacement, of jumping from one period to the other, that encourages the viewer "to see and hear our own world in a fresh way." She said the idea for the film came to her as a series of black-and-white images, in 1984. First aired on PBS, *Book of Days* played film festivals from Hong Kong to Montreal, before being released commercially. It was shown at the Whitney Museum's Biennial in New York, in 1991.

Although Monk has been calling her large-scale works "operas" since the early 1970s, her use of the word was always more as a descriptive term, meant to designate the "multi-perceptual, mosaic form" she always envisioned her music taking. Consequently, in the mid-1980s when she spoke with David Gockley, general director of the Houston Grand Opera, about writing a work using classically trained voices, it was her first opportunity to create an actual opera. The result, *Atlas: An Opera in Three Parts*—a co-commission by the Houston Grand Opera, the Walker Arts Center in Minneapolis, and the American Music Theater Festival in Philadelphia—was premiered in Houston in February 1991. In many respects, it brings together into one work most of the ideas, themes, and forms that have been important to Monk throughout her career. She said she started work on *Atlas* in the summer of 1987, while a resident at the MacDowell Colony, an artist's retreat in New Hampshire. As usual, her process was intuitive. In describing how work on the opera actually began, Monk said, "When shards of music suggested themselves to me, I developed them without knowing exactly where they would appear in the overall form."

On a larger scale, Monk wrote *Atlas* the same way she writes all her material. Her method, as she has described it, begins as trial and error, "translating certain concepts, images and energies" into her voice, seeing how they feel, how they sound. Slowly, she refines each idea into a musical form. From there, she begins to transfer the music to her ensemble, testing and developing each piece through extended group improvisations. Monk says she has learned not to commit any of her music to paper until she has performed it for a while; in these early stages it keeps constantly changing. She also says she has learned to keep her instrumental writing "simple and transparent," since this leaves her room—"aural space," she calls it—for her more complex solo or thickly textured vocal ensemble sounds. In *Atlas*, she limited the size of her orchestra to chamber ensemble proportions, saying she did this in order to "explore in depth the colors and textures" of each instrument.

Monk on the Value of Art

I always feel that what I try to do in my work is to offer to an audience new ways of seeing or hearing things that they might take for granted. So that when you leave, you might go out in the street and experience it in a new way because you've opened up certain kinds of perceptions or feelings in the concert.

Talking Music, 1995

The story of *Atlas* centers on the life of Alexandra Daniels, a character portrayed by Monk, and inspired by Alexandra David-Neel, an explorer and the first woman from the West to reach Tibet. In a three-part narrative, subdivided into twenty-four scenes, Monk traces Alexandra's search for self—accompanied by four explorer companions and taught by Spiritual Guides—from her earliest memory (the smell of coffee), to her teenage years in a suburban home, on through the worldwide adventures of her quest, and, finally, to her attainment of the realm of pure knowledge, energy, and light. Along the way, the five explorers circle the globe, each undergoing trials that test their inner resources. Eventually, the four survivors ascend to a radiant place of light, filled with the spiritual knowledge they had been seeking. And in the end, Alexandra returns full circle, older and wiser, sitting quietly drinking coffee in her home.

Surprising as it may seem, very little of Meredith Monk's vocal music actually uses words. And *Atlas*, even though it is an opera, is no exception. As always, Monk relies on tones of voice and inflection, combined with subtle movement and staging, to infuse her wordless melodies with a sense of understanding. K. Robert Schwarz said that while the effect of an opera without words was "eerie," the eighteen singers in *Atlas* produced "a wordless lyricism of such elemental resonance that its meaning is clear." He compared the experience to hearing a foreign language for the first time, yet understanding every word. The *New York Times*, on the other hand, called *Atlas* an opera that "only a choreographer could have conceived." Monk's response was that she has always felt that "the voice itself is a language." She said her plan in *Atlas* was "to bypass discursive thought and go directly to the heart."

Although Meredith Monk's music has always been difficult to categorize, it is, as Laura Shapiro said in *Newsweek*, "among the friendliest and most accessible of any in the avant-garde." This, too, is true for *Atlas*. Following it's successful premiere in Houston, Monk's opera played Minneapolis, Philadelphia, and Columbus, Ohio, before embarking on a European tour. The first New York performance was given in 1992 at the Brooklyn Academy of Music, and ECM released the recording the following year. In 1995, Monk, who has received numerous honors throughout her career—two Guggenheims, three Obies, a recent American Dance Festival award, to name a few—became a certified "genius," the recipient of a John D. and Catherine T. MacArthur Foundation fellowship. It didn't change her dedication to her work.

If there is a common denominator that runs through all of Monk's music, it is that she is an artist who works with feelings suspended in time. The sense of timelessness—of time going in a circle—that she tries to create in all of her work, is there not only for entertainment, but because she thinks it helps people to reevaluate and improve their lives. She once told *Newsweek* magazine that she thought our present-day society was "systematically eliminating feelings and shades of feelings" from our lives, but that she was confident that art could "still give people an intense emotional experience," one that could actually help them change. Recently, she said she thinks it is very important that artists keep working, even in the face of economic uncertainty, "because what we do is not covered by anything else." As she says, "There are certain things that technology does very well . . . and it feeds certain parts of human beings. But I think that the heart and soul are not covered that much, and that art can do that." For her, "art is an affirmation of human life, and an alternative to certain kinds of behavior." In 1996, Monk told the *New York Times* that she believes in the healing power of art.

Afterword

In the fall of 1997, the *New York Times* asked Meredith Monk to interview Merce Cunningham, as a preview for the opening of his dance company's new season at the Brooklyn Academy of Music. As they talked and reminisced, Monk worried that, in stimulating times such as these, "it's easy to lose touch with silence and stillness," asking, "Is this a generation that can't tolerate quietness . . . because they are so accustomed to speed?" Cunningham thought maybe that was so, but said he wasn't worried, because there would always be something to make people realize "that there's a whole other area to explore" out there.

In some ways, that's where we, as listeners, are now; ready for those other areas to explore. As you continue to listen to the music of this century and beyond, it might help to remember two other things Monk said to Cunningham during their talk. The first was that she is a gardener, and that watching her plants come up every year makes her realize how many truly different aspects of creativity there are. The other concerned her feeling that it was wonderful doing things she hadn't been trained in, "because you have your own vision and not a lot of preconceived notions about what you're supposed to do." Cunningham's response was, "And it doesn't matter if you're right or wrong." As you continue your exploration of new music from here, remember that there is no "right" way to listen to and learn about twentieth-century music. Follow your ear. Have fun.

THE LONG LIST

This is the complete list of pieces I made from the original lists of 20. It contains 86 works, written by 57 different composers.

Year	Work	Composer
1894	Prelude to the Afternoon of a Faun	Claude Debussy
1899	Maple Leaf Rag	Scott Joplin
1902	Shéhérazade	Maurice Ravel
1904	Thanksgiving	Charles Ives
1905	La Mer	Claude Debussy
1906	The Unanswered Question	Charles Ives
1909	Das Lied von der Erde (Die Absehied)	Gustav Mahler
1909	First Piano Sonata	Charles Ives
1910	Preludes for Piano, Book I	Claude Debussy
1912	Three Places in New England	Charles Ives
1912	Pierrot Lunaire	Arnold Schoenberg
1913	The Rite of Spring	Igor Stravinsky
1915	The Concord Sonata	Charles Ives
1923	Aeolian Harp	Henry Cowell
1924	Ballet Mecanique	George Antheil
1924	Rhapsody in Blue	George Gershwin
1926	Suite on Danish Folk-Songs	Percy Grainger
1928	Bolero	Maurice Ravel
1928	String Quartet No. 4	Béla Bartók
1930	Symphony of Psalms	Igor Stravinsky
1931	Ionisation	Edgard Varèse
1931	Piano Concerto No. 2	Béla Bartók

1931	Sun Treader	Carl Ruggles
1934	Four Saints in Three Acts	Virgil Thomson
1935	Porgy and Bess	George Gershwin
1935	Ricercar, from the Musical Offering	Anton Webern (Bach)
1935	Sinfonia India	Carlos Chávez
1935	Violin Concerto	Alban Berg
1936	Music for Strings, Percussion and Celeste	Bèla Bartók
1936	Piano Variations	Anton Webern
1938	Alexander Nevsky	Serge Prokofiev
1941	Quartet for the End of Time	Oliver Messiaen
1944	3 Short Liturgies of the Divine Presence	Oliver Messiaen
1944	Appalachian Spring	Aaron Copland
1948	Sonatas and Interludes	John Cage
1948	Turangalila	Oliver Messiaen
1948–93	Studies for Player Piano, Nos. 1–50	Conlon Nancarrow
1952	4´33″	John Cage
1955	Mysterious Mountain	Alan Hovhaness
1957	Zyklus	Karlheinz Stockhausen
1957	West Side Story	Leonard Bernstein
1958	Aria	John Cage
1960	Circles	Luciano Berio
1960	Threnody to the Victims of Hiroshima	Krzysztof Penderecki
1960s	Volumina	Gyorgy Ligeti
1961	Atmospheres	Gyorgy Ligeti
1964	In C	Terry Riley
1964	Philomel	Milton Babbitt
1964	The Well-Tuned Piano	La Monte Young
1966	Come Out	Steve Reich
1966	Delusion of the Fury	Harry Partch
1966	On the 7th Day Petals Fell in Petaluma	Harry Partch
1967	November Steps	Toru Takemitsu
1968	A Rainbow in Curved Air	Terry Riley
1968	The Wild Bull	Morton Subotnick
1968	Nomos Alpha	Yannis Xenakis
1969	Music in Similar Motion	Philip Glass
1969	Night of the 4 Moons	George Crumb
1970	I Am Sitting in a Room	Alvin Lucier
1970	Piano Transplants	Annea Lockwood
1970	Mantra	Karlheinz Stockhausen

1971	Drumming	Steve Reich
1972	Speech Songs	Charles Dodge
1973	4th String Quartet, Amazing Grace	Ben Johnston
1973	Songs and Views from the Magic Garden	Alvin Curran
1974	Appalachian Grove	Laurie Spiegel
1975	The People United Will Never Be Defeated	Frederic Rzewski
1975	Rituel	Pierre Boulez
1976	Einstein on the Beach	Philip Glass
1976	Music for 18 Musicians	Steve Reich
1977	Symphony of Sorrowful Songs	Henryk Gorecki
1977	Kottos	Yannis Xenakis
1978	Shaker Loops	John Adams
1981	Koyaanisqatsi	Philip Glass
1981	Tehillim	Steve Reich
1982	Ellis Island	Meredith Monk
1982	Passio	Arvo Pärt
1983	Perfect Lives	Robert Ashley
1983	United States (O Superman)	Laurie Anderson
1983	Wild Women With Steak Knives	Diamanda Galas
1987	for Samuel Beckett	Morton Feldman
1988	Early Winter	Phill Niblock
1989	Miserere	Arvo Pärt
1991	Atlas	Meredith Monk
1992	Improvement (Don Leaves Linda)	Robert Ashley

Time Line

Music, People, and Events

1813		Wagner born
1862		Debussy born
1866		Satie born
1868		Joplin born
1874		Ives born
		Schoenberg born
1875		Ravel born
1876	Mallarmé's poem *Afternoon of a Faun* published	
	Wagner's theater in Bayreuth opens	
1882		Stravinsky born
1883		Wagner dies
1884	Debussy wins *Prix de Rome*	
1889		Paris World Exhibition

1893	World's Columbian Exposition in Chicago
1894	**Debussy's** *Prelude to the Afternoon of a Faun* **premiered in Paris**
	Joplin settles in Sedalia, Missouri
1898	Gershwin born
1899	Joplin's *Maple Leaf Rag* published
1900	Copland born
1906	U. S. Marine Band records *Maple Leaf Rag*
1907	Joplin moves to New York
	Messiaen born
1909	First appearance of the Ballet Russes in Paris
1911	Hovhaness born
1912	Ballet Russes dances Debussy's *Prelude to the Afternoon of a Faun* in Paris
	Cage born
	Schoenberg's *Pierrot Lunaire* **premiered in Berlin**
1913	**Stravinsky's** *The Rite of Spring* **premiered in Paris**

1914		World War I begins
1915	**Ives completes** **_The Concord Sonata_**	
		Ford begins producing Model T cars
1916	Joplin makes a hand-played piano roll of _Maple Leaf Rag_ in New York	
1917	Joplin dies	
		U.S. declares war on Germany
	Schoenberg founds the Society for the Private Performance of Music	
1918	Debussy dies	
		World War I ends
	Stravinsky begins writing in a neoclassical style	
1921	Schoenberg invents the 12-tone technique	
	Copland studies in France with Boulanger	
1924	**_Rhapsody in Blue_** **premiered in New York** **by Paul Whiteman's Band**	
1925	Satie dies	
1926	Johnston born	

1927		First successful demonstration of television in New York City
1929		the stock market crash
1928	**Bolero danced by Ida Rubinstein at the Paris Opera**	
1930		Ashley born
1931		Lucier born
1935		Riley born
		Pärt born
1936		Reich born
1937		Gershwin dies
		Ravel dies
		Glass born
1939	**Ives's Concord Sonata premiered in New York by John Kirkpatrick**	
1940	Walt Disney uses *The Rite of Spring* in *Fantasia*	
	Cage writes *Bacchanale*, his first piece for prepared piano	
1941		World War II begins
1942		Monk born

**Messiaen's *Quartet
for the End of Time*
premiered in Stalag 8A**

1944   **Copland's *Appalachian
Spring* premiered in Washington**

1945   World War II ends

Copland awarded
a Pulitzer Prize

1946   Ives elected to
membership in the
National Institute of
Arts and Letters

First electronic
digital computer

1947   Ives awarded
a Pulitzer Prize

Anderson born

1948   Long-playing
record introduced

1949   Messiaen teaches a
summer course in
composition at Tanglewood

**Cage's *Sonatas and Interludes*
premiered in New York**

Cage receives awards from the
Guggenheim Foundation and the
National Institute of Arts and Letters

1950   Cage begins using *I Ching* chance
operations to compose music

1951   Schoenberg dies

1952	Stravinsky adopts the 12-tone style of Arnold Schoenberg	
	Cage writes his silent piece, *4´33˝*	
1954	Ives dies	
1955	**Hovhaness's *Mysterious Mountain* premiered in Houston, Texas**	
1957		First earth satellite launched by the Soviet Union
1960		President Kennedy assassinated
1962	Pärt's *Nekrolog* criticized at the Third All-Union Congress of Composers in Moscow	
1963	Glass studies in France with Boulanger	
1964	**Riley's *In C* premiered in San Francisco**	
		The Beatles make their first U.S. tour
1965	Lucier writes first piece to use brain waves as a compositional element	
1969		U.S. astronauts walk on the moon
		Woodstock

Riley performs at
The Electric Circus
in New York

1970   Reich travels to
Ghana to study
African drumming

**Lucier's *I Am Sitting
in a Room* premiered
in New York**

1971   **Reich's *Drumming*
premiered in New York**

                     Stravinsky dies

1973   end of the
Vietnam War

1974   **Johnston's *String
Quartet No. 4,
Amazing Grace*
premiered in New York**

1975   Anderson invents
the tape bow violin

1976   **Glass's *Einstein on
the Beach* premiered
at the Avignon Festival**

Pärt ends a seven-year
silence with the invention
of his "tintinnabuli" style

Joplin awarded a special
Bicentennial Pulitzer Prize

1978   The Kitchen commissions
Ashley to create an opera
for television

Monk founds
her Vocal Ensemble

1980 Pärt and his family
emigrate to the West

1981 Anderson's "O Superman"
rises to No. 2 on the British
rock singles chart

1982   compact discs
                                                  introduced

1983 **Anderson's *United States,***
Parts 1–4 premiered
in New York

Joplin postage stamp
issued by the
U.S. Postal Service

1984 **Ashley's *Perfect Lives***
premiered on British television

1985 Glass named
Musical America's
Musician of the Year

1986 **Early version of Pärt's**
***Miserere* premiered in Rouen**

1988 Glass commissioned
by the Metropolitan Opera
to write *The Voyage*

1989 Pärt completes
the *Miserere*

1990   Copland dies

1991 Pärt's *Miserere*
released by ECM Records

1991 **Monk's *Atlas* premiered by
the Houston Grand Opera**

1992 Messiaen dies

Cage dies

1995 Monk receives a
MacArthur Foundation
Fellowship

Sources

General

Austin, William. *Music in the 20th Century.* New York: Norton, 1966.

Chase, Gilbert. *America's Music.* Rev. 2d ed. New York: McGraw-Hill, 1955, 1966.

Duckworth, William. *Talking Music.* New York: Schirmer Books, 1995.

Fisk, Josiah, ed. *Composers on Music.* Boston: Northeastern University Press, 1956, 1997.

Gagne, Cole, and Tracy Caras. *Soundpieces: Interviews with American Composers.* Metuchen, N.J., & London: Scarecrow, 1982. Composers interviewed include Robert Ashley, John Cage, Aaron Copland, Philip Glass, Ben Johnston, and Steve Reich.

Kostelanetz, Richard. *On Innovative Music(ian)s.* New York: Limelight Editions, 1989. Includes chapters on Charles Ives, John Cage, Alan Hovhaness, and Philip Glass.

Rockwell, John. *All American Music: Composition in the Late Twentieth Century.* New York: Knopf, 1983. A group of twenty essays, each constructed around one composer or ensemble. The composers range from Milton Babbitt to Ornette Coleman, and include Laurie Anderson, Philip Glass, Robert Ashley, and John Cage.

Slonimsky, Nicolas. *Lexicon of Musical Invection, Critical Assaults on Composers since Beethoven's Time.* 2d ed. Seattle: University of Washington Press, 1953, 1965.

Strickland, Edward. *American Composers: Dialogues on Contemporary Music.* Bloomington: Indiana University Press, 1991. Contains interviews with Terry Riley, Steve Reich, Philip Glass, and Meredith Monk, among others.

Sumner, Melody, Kathleen Burch, and Michael Sumner, eds. *The Guests Go in to Supper*. Oakland, CA: Burning Books, 1986. A compilation of the texts, scores, and ideas of seven American composers who use words as an integral part of their compositions, including Laurie Anderson, Robert Ashley, and John Cage.

Vinton, John, ed. *Dictionary of Contemporary Music.* New York: Dutton, 1974.

By Composer

CLAUDE DEBUSSY

If you want to know more about Debussy's *Prelude to the Afternoon of a Faun*, the best single source is *Debussy, Prelude to "The Afternoon of a Faun"* (New York: Norton, 1970). This volume of the Norton Critical Scores, edited by William W. Austin, contains a translation of Mallarmé's poem, a score of the work, and essays on background, sources, criticism, and analysis.

Symbolist poetry, with all its shadows and half-lights, is difficult to translate and any two versions of Mallarmé, for example, may vary more than you would think. My own particular favorite for a translation of *Afternoon of a Faun*, and the one I quote from, is by Hayden Carruth (Tucson: Ironwood Press, 1981), himself a poet.

Debussy wrote music criticism from 1901 to 1914, for such publications as *Gil Blas, Le Figaro*, and *S.I.M.* He even invented a fictitious character—M. Croche, anti-dilettante—to discuss things with in print. These writings have been collected by François Lesure, and translated into English by Richard Langham Smith, as *Debussy on Music* (Ithaca, NY: Cornell University Press, 1988). Many of the quotes in both the text and the sidebars come from here.

The most thorough biography on Debussy's life and work is the two-volume set by Edward Lockspeiser, *Debussy: His Life and Mind* (London, 1963). Another, which is more readily found in bookstores today, is Leon Vallas's *Claude Debussy, His Life and Works* (New York: Dover, 1973). Originally published in 1933, Vallas knew Debussy and writes with authority about him and his work. A more popular, but well-written, book is Paul Holmes, *Debussy* in The Illustrated Lives of the Great Composers series (London: Omnibus Press, 1989).

SCOTT JOPLIN

The single best source for information on the life of Scott Joplin, is Edward A. Berlin's *King of Ragtime: Scott Joplin and His Era* (New York: Oxford University Press, 1994). Many of the quotes I've used come from here.

For a good general discussion of ragtime, complete with lots of interviews with people who should know, see Rudi Blesh and Harriet Janis's *They All Played Ragtime* (New York: Knopf, 1950; 4th ed., New York: Oak, 1971). This book spearheaded the seventies ragtime revival.

If you play piano you will find Rudi Blesh's compilation *Classic Piano Rags* (New York: Dover, 1973), a gold mine of early rags.

A second edition of *The Complete Works of Scott Joplin*, edited by Vera Brodsky Lawrence, was published by the New York Public Library in 1981.

IGOR STRAVINSKY

Stravinsky wrote extensively about his work. Unfortunately, he also engaged in a bit of revisionist history, particularly in his later writings. For that reason, I relied mainly on two of his earliest books, *Stravinsky: An Autobiography* (New York: Simon & Schuster, 1936), and *Poetics of Music* (Cambridge, MA: Harvard University Press, 1942). The latter is a series of lectures he gave at Harvard shortly after emigrating to the United States.

The score to *The Rite of Spring* is available both for full orchestra (Kalmus or Dover), and in a reduction for piano duet (Boosey & Hawkes). The Dover edition, published in 1989, is a republication of the edition originally published by the State Music Publishing House in Moscow in 1965, and contains an interesting foreword by Boris Mikhailovich Yarustovsky in which he calls Stravinsky "an authentic magician of the modern orchestra."

The amount of material available on Stravinsky is enormous. To date, over 900 books about him have been written, more than 700 of which are in English. Of these, the most comprehensive, particularly as it relates to his Russian period, is Richard Taruskin's *Stravinsky and the Russian Traditions* (Berkeley: University of California Press, 1996), a two-volume set of more than 1,700 pages, about which *The New York Times Book Review* said, "There is no parallel in musical scholarship".

The book I quoted in the text and relied on for many of the facts is Andre Boucourechliev's *Stravinsky* translated by Martin Cooper (New York: Holmes & Meier, 1987).

Stravinsky in Pictures and Documents by Vera Stravinsky and Robert Craft (New York: Simon & Schuster, 1978) is an excellent source of documents, pictures, letters, and text prepared by Stravinsky's second wife, Vera, and his closest associate, Robert Craft.

The Voyager CD-Rom, *Stravinsky, The Rite of Spring*, by Robert Winter includes the sound of the music, a copy of the score, and many facts and details about the music and the first performance in Paris.

ARNOLD SCHOENBERG

The best place to begin unraveling the complicated ideas of Arnold Schoenberg is with his own writings. *Style and Idea: Selected Writings of Arnold Schoenberg*, edited by Leonard Stein (Berkeley and Los Angeles: University of California Press, 1984), is an expanded version of a work first published in 1950, that collects most of Schoenberg's articles, essays, and speeches into one volume. His "Composition with 12-Tones," first delivered as a lecture at the University of California at Los Angeles in 1941, is must reading.

Although there are a number of books on Schoenberg, my favorite, from which I quote occasionally, is Charles Rosen's *Arnold Schoenberg* (Chicago: University of

Chicago Press, 1975). As Jonathan Dunsby characterizes it, it is "short and simply written, is the outstanding account of what it is that makes this composer a 'modern master', and is particularly interesting about the atonal works".

For fans of *Pierrot Lunaire,* Jonathan Dunsby's *Schoenberg: Pierrot lunaire* (Cambridge: Cambridge University Press, 1992) is a must. A paperback in the Cambridge Music Handbooks series, it explores the image of Pierrot, the milieu of Schoenberg's emotional and professional lives, and each of the twenty-one songs individually. The portrait that emerges is of a very complex and complicated man indeed.

CHARLES IVES

If you've never read any of the transcendentalist writers, this might be a good time to begin. They were all the rage in mid-nineteenth-century America, taken as gospel by some. For Ives's own unique interpretation of them, as well as his thoughts on *The Concord Sonata* and music in general, his *Essays Before a Sonata and Other Writings,* edited by Howard Boatwright (New York: Norton, 1962), is indispensable. Also interesting, though less organized, are Ives's memos from the early 1930s, edited by John Kirkpatrick as *Charles E. Ives: Memos* (New York: Norton, 1972).

I relied extensively on *Charles Ives and His Music* by Henry and Sidney Cowell (New York: Oxford University Press, 1955), the first book on Ives, written by his friends with his cooperation, and published only a year after his death. More recent books, of which there are many, give deeper insight into various aspects of his life and work, but none give the feeling of the person quite so clearly. Also useful were the lavishly illustrated Program Booklet of the 100th Anniversary Record Box (New York: CBS, Inc., 1974), and *Charles Ives Remembered: An Oral History* by Vivian Perlis (New York: Norton, 1976).

GEORGE GERSHWIN

There were a number of tributes following Gershwin's death in 1937. None was more significant, or more lasting, than Merle Armitage's *George Gershwin* (New York: Longman, Green, 1938; Da Capo Press edition, 1995), a memorial collection of thirty-eight essays, articles, and remembrances by friends, collaborators, and celebrities. Twenty-six essays were written in the year following Gershwin's death, while twelve are reprints of articles published during his lifetime. The contributors include his brother, Ira, Paul Whiteman, and Arnold Schoenberg. Two previously published pieces by Gershwin himself are included. Most of the quotes I use in the text come from either this collection or the following.

An equally important contribution to Gershwin scholarship (also containing quotes, but not entire essays from Armitage) is Edward Jablonski's *Gershwin Remembered* (Portland, OR: Amadeus Press, 1992). It is a collection of factual information and quotes, and concludes with a selection of Gershwin's own comments about music, jazz, and his own compositions.

MAURICE RAVEL

Maurice Ravel is confusing, and difficult to understand. Although I began this chapter thinking I knew a lot about him, the more I learned, the more I found I needed to know. Consequently, I did a lot of reading, beginning with Roland-Manuel's *Maurice Ravel* (London: Dennis Dobson Limited, 1947; first published in France in 1938). Roland-Manuel was Ravel's first pupil, then his friend, and, later, his first biographer. He was in a position to know Ravel as well as anyone could.

For more up-to-date information on Ravel, I turned to Gerald Larner's *Maurice Ravel* (London: Phaidon Press Limited, 1996), another of their Twentieth-Century Composers series. I also consulted H. H. Stuckenschmidt's *Maurice Ravel* (Philadelphia: Chilton Book Company, 1968; first published in Germany in 1966).

Arbie Orenstein's *A Ravel Reader* (New York: Columbia University Press, 1990) is a welcome collection of Ravel's correspondence, articles, and interviews. If you want to know what Ravel said, here is the place to find out. Orenstein's earlier book *Ravel: Man and Musician* (New York: Columbia University Press, 1968, 1975) has been reissued (New York, Dover Publications, Inc., 1991). It, too, is a wealth of information.

OLIVIER MESSIAEN

For anyone wishing to know what Messiaen may have said on any particular subject, Claude Samuel's *Oliver Messiaen: Music and Color* (Portland, OR: Amadeus Press, 1994) is the place to go. In a series of conversations first published in France in1986, and translated into English by E. Thomas Glasow, Messiaen discusses his techniques, his search for new rhythms, and the relationship of sounds and colors. The majority of my Messiaen quotes come from here.

The most thorough study of Messiaen is Robert Sherlaw Johnson's *Messiaen* (London: Dent, 1975). This survey of all of Messiaen's music discusses his various compositional techniques, illustrating them with music examples. Although not as complete, Carla Huston Bell's *Olivier Messiaen* (Boston: Twayne, 1984) clearly discusses Messiaen's techniques, and has the advantage of devoting an entire chapter to an analysis of the *Quartet for the End of Time*.

For those who wish to explore Messiaen's techniques in even more detail, his own *Technique de mon langage musical* (2 vols.) (Paris: Alphonse Leduc & Cie., 1944), English translation by John Satterfield, *The Technique of My Musical Language* (Paris: Alphonse Leduc & Cie., 1956) is the place to start. It analyzes his work from that period, drawing heavily for examples from the *Quartet for the End of Time*. Messiaen said he wrote the book to satisfy the questions of his students.

AARON COPLAND

Unlike many composers, Copland was a prolific writer of words as well as music. His books *What to Listen for in Music* (New York: Whittlesey House, 1939); *Our New Music* (New York: Whittlesey House, 1941), with its autobiographical chapter

"Composer from Brooklyn"; and *Music and Imagination* (Cambridge, MA: Harvard University Press, 1952), originally Copland's Charles Elliott Norton lectures at Harvard, yield continual insights into the mind of the composer.

The last, and most informative of the books to which Copland personally contributed is Aaron Copland and Vivian Perlis's *Copland: Since 1943* (New York: St. Martin's, 1989). With its companion first volume, *Copland: 1900 Through 1942*, this definitive autobiography is the place to go for information, photographs, and remembrances by friends and colleagues.

For my own use, I found Arthur Berger's *Aaron Copland* (New York: Oxford University Press, 1953) both useful and insightful. Berger, a composer himself, knew Copland in the early 1930s when he became a member of the Young Composers Group, and they remained friends and colleagues. His book is developed from articles on Copland he wrote for *The Musical Quarterly* and *Tempo*.

JOHN CAGE

The best source for material on Cage is his own writings. His first book, *Silence* (Middletown, CT: Wesleyan University Press, 1961), is a collection of his early writings and lectures, covering both his music and his aesthetic ideas, and including his thoughts on Zen, indeterminacy, and chance music. *A Year from Monday* (Middletown, 1967) includes the additional lectures and writings produced between 1961 and 1967. More diary-like than *Silence*, it contains Cage's thoughts on Zen, botany, his own music, and his comments on other artists such as Ives, Jasper Johns, and Marcel Duchamp. *M: Writings '67–'72* (Middletown, 1973) is more poetic in nature than his previous books, containing experiments with typography, additional diary entries, and "Mureau," a mix of letters, syllables, words, phrases, and sentences chosen by chance from the remarks of Henry David Thoreau on music. The title, "Mureau," comes from the first syllable of the word music and the last syllable of Thoreau. *Empty Words: Writings '73–78* (Middletown, 1979) contains the text-sound piece "Empty Words," as well as pieces on "How the Piano Came to be Prepared" and "The Future of Music."

Of the books about Cage, of which there are many, those by Richard Kostelanetz deserve special mention. Kostelanetz is the most consistent chronicler of Cage's life and work. His first book, *John Cage* (1970; rev. ed. New York: Da Capo, 1991), is a collection of mostly short pieces by and about Cage from the earliest parts of his career. Kostelanetz's more recent books include *John Cage (ex)plain(ed)* (New York: Schirmer Books, 1996), *John Cage Writer: Previously Uncollected Pieces* (New York: Limelight Editions, 1993), and *Writings About John Cage* (Ann Arbor: University of Michigan Press, 1993).

ALAN HOVHANESS

At present, there are still no book-length studies of Alan Hovhaness or his work, but several books do include chapters on him. Of these, the best is Richard Kostelanetz's *On Innovative Music(ian)s* (New York: Limelight Editions, 1989). Written in 1979, it is based on an interview Kostelanetz did with Hovhaness in Seattle in 1977. David Ewen's *American Composers: A Biographical Dictionary* (New York: Putnam's, 1982) also contains a chapter on Hovhaness, but as the title of the book suggests, it is written in the style of a dictionary entry.

Of the interviews and articles in magazines, the best I have found is Peter Westbrook's "Alan Hovhaness: Angelic Cycles" in *Down Beat* (March 1982). Although short, Westbrook's interview is both clear and revealing. Also short but interesting is Don Gillespie and Charlie Morrow's "Interview with Alan Hovhaness" in *Ear Magazine* (July/August 1984). The magazine is long out of print, but larger libraries may have a copy. A longer interview with Hovhaness, but focused primarily on his choral writing, is Vance D. Wolverton's "From Mountain Climbing to Composing: An Interview with Alan Hovhaness" in *The Choral Journal* (October 1993). It concludes with a list of Hovhaness's published choral music.

TERRY RILEY

At present, there are no book-length studies of Terry Riley or his work. There is, however, K. Robert Schwarz's *Minimalists* (London: Phaidon Press Limited, 1996). One of the Twentieth-Century Composers series edited by Norman Lebrecht, Schwarz's book includes lengthy discussions of not only Terry Riley, but minimalists Steve Reich, Philip Glass, and Meredith Monk.

Also, a number of interviews with Riley are in print, including Edward Strickland's *American Composers: Dialogues on Contemporary Music* (Bloomington: Indiana University Press, 1991), from which I took several quotes by Riley, and my own *Talking Music* (New York: Schirmer Books, 1995).

Riley has also been interviewed for a number of magazines, among the best of which is Patricia and Joseph Mancini's, "On Just Intonation, Melodic Inflection, and the Spiritual Source of Music: Terry Riley" in *Keyboard* (July 1986).

STEVE REICH

The best source of information on Steve Reich's earliest minimalist music is his own *Writings about Music* (Halifax, N.S., Canada: The Press of the Nova Scotia College of Art and Design, 1974). In addition to his 1968 essay "Music as a Gradual Process," it contains sections on African and Balinese music, "Notes on the Ensemble" from 1973, and "Notes on Compositions."

In addition, K. Robert Schwarz's *Minimalists* (London: Phaidon Press Limited, 1996) devotes two chapters to Reich, and both Edward Strickland's *American Composers: Dialogues on Contemporary Music* (Bloomington: Indiana University Press, 1991) and my own *Talking Music* (New York: Schirmer Books, 1995) contain interviews with Reich.

ALVIN LUCIER

There are two books that explore the music of Alvin Lucier in some detail. The first is Alvin Lucier and Douglas Simon's *Chambers* (Middletown, CT: Wesleyan

University Press, 1980). It includes scores and interviews about many of Lucier's early works through the 1970s, including *Chambers, Vespers, I Am Sitting in a Room*, and *Music on a Long Thin Wire*. A more recent book, available from Germany, is Alvin Lucier's *Reflections: Interviews, Scores, Writings* (Koln: Edition MusikTexte, 1995). It contains much of the material from Lucier and Simon's *Chambers*, plus additional interviews, scores, and writings through 1993, in both English and German translation.

BEN JOHNSTON

At present, there is only one book on the music of Ben Johnston, Heidi Von Gunden's *The Music of Ben Johnston* (Metuchen, NJ, & London: Scarecrow, 1986). It contains chapters on Johnston's early years, his experiments with serialism and just intonation, and his adoption of extended just intonation, plus a chronology and catalog of compositions. Several books contain extended interviews with Johnston, including Gagne and Caras's *Soundpieces: Interviews With American Composers* (Metuchen, NJ, and London: Scarecrow, 1982) and my own *Talking Music* (New York: Schirmer Books, 1995). For an in-depth discussion of Johnston's Fourth Quartet, see Randall Shinn's "Ben Johnston's Fourth String Quartet," *Perspectives of New Music* 15, no. 2 (Spring–Summer, 1977).

PHILIP GLASS

Any additional reading on Philip Glass should begin with his own book *Music by Philip Glass* (New York: Harper & Row, 1987) in which he discusses his three portrait operas *Einstein on the Beach, Satyagraha*, and *Akhnaten*. Also of special interest is Richard Kostelanetz and Robert Flemming's *Writings on Glass: Essays, Interviews, Criticism* (New York: Schirmer Books, 1997), which includes an Overview on Glass, plus sections on Instrumental Music and Music for Theater and Film, as well as an Endgame, which includes a bibliography, works and discography.

K. Robert Schwarz's *Minimalists* (London: Phaidon Press Limited, 1996) contains several chapters on Philip Glass, as well as the other minimalists. And a number of books contain extensive interviews with Glass, including Edward Strickland's *American Composers: Dialogues on Contemporary Music* (Bloomington: Indiana University Press, 1991); Cole Gagne and Tracy Caras's *Soundpieces: Interviews With American Composers* (Metuchen, N.J., & London: 1982); and my own *Talking Music* (New York: Schirmer Books, 1995).

ROBERT ASHLEY

The place where all the interrelatedness begins in Ashley's work is *Perfect Lives*, so the first place to go is his own *Perfect Lives: an opera* (New York/San Francisco: Archer Fields/Burning Books, 1991). It contains a synopsis of the opera, the complete libretto, and excerpts of Ashley, at Mills College in 1989, talking about his ideas and the actual making of the opera. Another interesting source for both information and libretto is *The Guests Go in to Supper* (Oakland, CA: Burning Books, 1986), edited and designed by Melody Sumner, Kathleen Burch, and Michael Sumner. Here Ashley is one of seven artists profiled through interviews and examples of their work. There are also a number of interviews with Ashley, including Gagne and Caras's, *Soundpieces: Interviews With American Composers* (Metuchen, NJ, and London: Scarecrow, 1982).

LAURIE ANDERSON

By this point, there are a number of sources on Laurie Anderson, although, surprisingly, most of them are in magazines and newspapers, rather than books. Even C. Carr's *On Edge: Performance at the End of the Twentieth Century* (Hanover and London: Wesleyan University Press, 1993) barely mentions Anderson. Two good sources for her ideas, however, are John Rockwell's *All American Music: Composition in the Late Twentieth Century* (New York: Knopf, 1983), which includes a chapter on Laurie Anderson; and *The Guests Go in to Supper*, edited by Melody Sumner, Kathleen Burch, and Michael Sumner (Oakland, CA: Burning Books, 1986), a compilation of the texts, scores, and ideas of seven American composers who use words as an integral part of their compositions, including Laurie Anderson, Robert Ashley, and John Cage.

Of the many interviews, I relied most heavily on one Anderson gave to Joshua Baer of *Musician Magazine* in April 1984, and my own from *Talking Music* (New York: Schirmer Books, 1995).

And for critical comments surrounding the premiere of *United States*, I relied on John Rockwell, *The New York Times* (February 6, 1983); Jennifer Allen, *New York* (February 14, 1983); Michael Walsh, *Time* (February 21, 1983); Jack Kroll, *Newsweek* (February 21, 1983); and Sally Banes, *The Village Voice* (February 22, 1983).

Laurie Anderson also wrote her own book, *United States* (New York: Harper & Row, 1983), but it is primarily pictures and text, rather than an analysis, or an expansion, on the work.

ARVO PÄRT

The only comprehensive study of Pärt currently available is Paul Hillier's *Arvo Pärt* (Oxford and New York: Oxford University Press, 1997), one of the Oxford Studies of Composers series. Hillier, who first met Pärt in the early 1980s—and has conducted many of his works under supervision by the composer while director of the Hilliard Ensemble—brings an in-depth understanding to Pärt and his music. Most of my facts and many of the quotes came from here. Hillier's book is indispensable for anyone wishing to fully understand Pärt's "tintinnabuli" style.

K. Robert Schwarz's *Minimalists* (London: Phaidon Press Limited,1996) devotes a portion of a chapter to a discussion of Pärt. And of the interviews, of which there aren't that many, I found Martin Elste's "An Interview with Arvo Pärt," in *Fanfare* 11, no. 4 (March/April 1988), and Jamie McCarthy's "An Interview with Arvo Pärt," in *Musical Times* 130, no. 1753 (March 1989) the most helpful.

MEREDITH MONK

Meredith Monk, edited by Deborah Jowitt (Baltimore: Johns Hopkins University Press, 1997), is the best single source for information on Monk. It includes various articles and reviews, as well as some of Monk's own journal entries.

John Rockwell's *All American Music: Composition in the Late Twentieth Century* (New York: Knopf, 1983) contains a chapter on Monk, and K. Robert Schwarz's *Minimalists* (London: Phaidon Press Limited, 1996) devotes a part of a chapter to her work, although he doesn't think she is totally inside the minimalist camp. Of the interviews, of which there are many, I relied most heavily on Edward Strickland's *American Composers: Dialogues on Contemporary Music* (Bloomington: Indiana University Press, 1991) and my own *Talking Music* (New York: Schirmer Books, 1995).

INDEX

Index

Index

Paul Hillier, *Arvo Pärt*, © 1997 Oxford University Press. Reprinted by permission of Oxford University Press.

Notes from *Tabula Rosa* © 1980 Universal Edition AG, Vienna, ECM New Series 817 762-2 (1984)). Reprinted by permission of Oxford University Press.

Quotes from chapter 8, p. 62, "Quartet for the End of Time" (Olivier Messiaen) from *Olivier Messiaen: Music and Color* by Claude Samuel © 1986, 1994, published by Amadeus Press. Used by permission.

Quotes from chapter 6, p. 45, "Rhapsody in Blue" (George Gershwin) from *Gershwin Remembered*, © 1992, published by Amadeus Press. Used by permission.

Quotes from chapter 16, p. 134, "Einstein on the Beach" (Philip Glass): *Music by Philip Glass* by Philip Glass. Copyright © 1987 by Dunvagen Music Publishers, Inc. Used by permission of HarperCollins Publishers, Inc.

Excerpts from *Essays Before a Sonata, The Majority and Other Writings by Charles Ives* by Charles Ives edited by Howard Boatwright. Copyright © 1961, 1962 by W. W. Norton & Company, Inc., renewed 1990. Reprinted by permission of W. W. Norton & Company, Inc.

I Am Sitting in a Room by Alvin Lucier from *Reflections/Reflexionen*, published by Muisik Texte, Cologne. Reprinted by permission of Alvin Lucier.

Excerpts from *Poetics of Music* by Igor Stravinsky. Copyright © 1942, 1947, 1970 by the President and Fellows of Harvard College. Reprinted by permission of Harvard University Press.

Excerpts from Richard Langham Smith, *Debussy on Music*. Ithaca, NY: Cornell University Press, 1988.

Excerpts from Edward A. Berlin, *King of Ragtime: Scott Joplin and His Era*. New York: Oxford University Press, 1994.

Excerpts from Merle Armitage, *George Gershwin*. New York: Longmans, Green & Co., 1938. Da Capo Press edition, 1995.

Excerpts from Arbie Orenstein, *A Ravel Reader*. New York: Columbia University Press, 1990.

Excerpts from Roland-Manual, *Maurice Ravel*. London: Dennis Dobson Limited, 1947.

Excerpt from Gerald Larner, *Maurice Ravel*. London: Phaidon Press Limited, 1996.

Excerpts on Terry Riley and Steve Reich from Edward Strickland, *American Composers: Dialogues on Contemporary Music*. Bloomington: Indiana University Press, 1991. Used by permission.

Joshua Baer, Laurie Anderson interview in *Musician* magazine, April 1984. Used by permission.

Excerpts from *O Superman* by Laurie Anderson for Difficult Music. Used by permission of Laurie Anderson.

Contents of Compact Disc Included With

William Duckworth

∽ 20/20 ∽

20 New Sounds of the 20th Century

ISBN 0-02-864864-1 (Book & CD)
CD MAY NOT BE RETURNED INDEPENDENTLY OF BOOK

All selections are excerpts except when indicated**

1 Debussy: Prelude to the Afternoon of a Faun
Royal Concertgebouw Orchestra/Carlo Maria Giulini
Excerpt: Beginning to end of A section
℗ 1995 Sony Classical GmbH

2 Joplin: Maple Leaf Rag**
Scott Joplin, piano roll
Courtesy of Biograph Records, Inc.

3 Stravinsky: The Rite of Spring
Cleveland Orchestra/Pierre Boulez
Excerpt: Sacrificial Dance**

4 Schoenberg: Pierrot Lunaire
Yvonne Minton, reciter;
Ensemble conducted by Pierre Boulez
Excerpt: Mondestrunken**
℗ 1978 Sony Music Entertainment Inc.

5 Schoenberg: Pierrot Lunaire
Yvonne Minton, reciter;
Ensemble conducted by Pierre Boulez
Excerpt: Der Mondfleck**
℗ 1978 Sony Music Enter

6 Ives: Piano Sonata 1840-60"
Alan Mandel, piano
Excerpt: The Alcotts**
Courtesy of Essex Enter

7 Gershwin: Rhapsod
Columbia Symphony O
piano & conductor
Excerpt: Beginning

8 Ravel: Bolero
Orchestre National de F
Excerpt: Beginning
℗ 1981 Sony Music Ent

9 Messiaen: Quartet
Chamber Music Northwest
Excerpt: Liturgie de cristal**
℗ 1986 Delos International, Inc.
Courtesy of Delos International, Inc.

10 Copland: Appalachian Spring
London Symphony Orchestra;
Aaron Copland, conductor
Excerpt: Beginning of Variations on a
Shaker Hymn, "Simple Gifts"

11 Cage: Sonata No. 5 for Prepared Piano**
Philipp Vandré, prepared piano
℗ 1996 Mode Records
Excerpted from the recording of the complete Sonatas and
Interludes for Prepared Piano by John Cage, performed
by Philipp Vandré on Mode Records, Mode 50.

12 Hovhaness: Symphony No. 2, "Mysterious Mountain"
Chicago Symphony Orchestra/Fritz Reiner
Excerpt: 2nd Movement—Double Fugue:
Moderato maestoso**
Courtesy of BMG Entertainment, The RCA Records
Label, Under License from BMG Special Products

13 Riley: In C
Terry Riley with members of the Center of the Creative
and Performing Arts in the State University of
New York at Buffalo
Excerpt: Beginning

14 Lucier: I Am Sitting in a Room
Alvin Lucier
Excerpt: 1st reading,** 12th version,** 24th version**
℗ 1980 Lovely Music Ltd.
Courtesy of Lovely Music Ltd.

15 Johnston: 4th String Quartet, "Amazing Grace"
Fine Arts Quartet
Excerpt: Beginning through 5th Variation
aro Records, Inc.

on the Beach
nsemble
ene 3, "Spaceship"
ic Entertainment Inc.

t Lives
ce; "Blue" Gene Tyranny, piano

y Music Ltd.

mble/Paul Hillier
g
rds GmbH
Records, under license from BMG

Wilbur Pauley, Randall Wong, Voices;
Orchestra conducted by Wayne Hankin
Excerpt: Overture (Out of Body 1)**
℗ 1993 ECM Records GmbH
Courtesy of ECM Records, under license from BMG
Special Products

Recordings of Steve Reich's *Drumming* and
Laurie Anderson's *O Superman*
were not available for inclusion on this compact disc

Copyright © 1999 Schirmer Books

Schirmer Books
1633 Broadway
New York, NY 10019